A TRILLION* CLICHÉS EVERY DAD WILL DO WHETHER THEY LIKE IT OR NOT.

A TO-DO LIST (OF SORTS)

DISCLAIMER

✕ ✕ ✕

LOOK, WE TRIED OUR BEST—BUT WE'RE
JUST A COUPLE OF OVERAMBITIOUS
DESIGNERS THAT SEEM TO LIKE PUTTING
THEMSELVES THROUGH HELL COMING UP
WITH ALL OF THIS STUFF.

SO WHILE WE TRIED OUR BEST TO
NOT MAKE ANY TYPOS, IT'S INEVITABLE
THAT WE MADE A FEW. PLEASE
DON'T YELL AT US.

AND, YES, WE'RE FULLY AWARE THAT
WE WOULDN'T BE HAVING THIS PROBLEM
IF WE HAD JUST GONE TO MEDICAL
SCHOOL—BUT THANKS FOR THE TIP DAD.

@ BRASSMONKEYGOODS

THIS BOOK IS DEDICATED TO
OUR DADS. WE COULDN'T HAVE
WRITTEN IT WITHOUT YOU GUYS.
YOU KNOW, BECAUSE OF THE
WHOLE 'EXISTING' THING THAT
YOU HELPED US OUT WITH.

X X X

WE LOVE YOU.

HOW TO USE THIS BOOK

A TUTORIAL

DADS ARE INTERESTING PEOPLE. THEY'RE LIKE GIANT, EMBARRASSING SNOWFLAKES. WHILE THEY ALL LOOK VAGUELY SIMILAR ON THE OUTSIDE, THEY'RE EACH UNIQUE..TO SAY THE LEAST.

SO WE MADE THIS QUASI TO-DO LIST AS OUR LITTLE WAY OF CELEBRATING WHAT OUR OWN DADS DID FOR US...GOOD, BAD, AND OUTRIGHT CRAZY. WE HOPE THAT IT BRINGS BACK FOND MEMORIES OF YOUR OWN FATHER (OR FATHER-FIGURE) AND GIVES YOU PLENTY OF FRESH IDEAS FOR WAYS TO COMPLETELY EMBARRASS YOUR OWN CHILDREN—IN THE MOST LOVING WAY POSSIBLE.

SO JUST GO THROUGH THE BOOK AND CHECK OFF THE ONES YOU'RE GUILTY OF (WHICH IS LIKELY MORE THAN YOU'LL CARE TO ADMIT), AND TAKE THE OPPORTUNITY TO EXECUTE ANY NEW 'IDEAS' THAT YOU DISCOVER.

JUST REMEMBER, THIS IS ALL IN GOOD FUN. DADS, EVEN WITH THE BEST INTENTIONS, HAVE SOME TERRIBLE IDEAS SOMETIMES. SO JUST BECAUSE WE LISTED SOMETHING IN HERE DOESN'T MEAN IT'S ACTUALLY A GOOD IDEA.

AS OUR DAD WOULD SAY, 'HAVE SOME COMMON SENSE.' NOW THAT WOULD BE FOLLOWED BY A FEW EXPLETIVES, BUT YOU GET THE IDEA.

IN THE BACK OF THE BOOK, WE'VE ALSO GIVEN YOU SOME SPACE TO WRITE DOWN ANY 'CLASSICS' THAT WE'VE MISSED—EITHER ONES THAT YOUR FATHER DID, OR SOME OF YOUR OWN PERSONAL CREATIONS. PSST: PLEASE SHARE SOME WITH US AT @ BRASSMONKEYGOODS. WE'D LOVE TO SEE THEM.

SEE THIS FINE PRINT? WELL, ANY GOOD DAD WOULD BE POINTING TO IT & SAYING SOMETHING LIKE 'THAT'S WHERE THEY GET YOU.' IN THIS CASE HOWEVER, WE'RE NOT TRYING TO SNEAK ANYTHING PAST YOU. WE JUST WANTED TO TAKE A MOMENT TO GIVE A SINCERE THANKS TO EVERY DAD OUT THERE—NOW PULL OUR FINGER.

MANDATORY DAD CLICHÉ · NO. 1

WHEN SOMETHING COSTS MORE THAN IT USED TO, PROCLAIM IT TO BE 'HIGHWAY ROBBERY.'

SIGNED WITNESS

COMPLETED SUCCESSFULLY ☐

YET TO DO ☐

CERTIFIED EXPERT ☐

NOW GIVE IT A REVIEW

☐ HIGHLY RECOMMENDED

☐ IT WAS ENJOYABLE

☐ NOT WORTH THE TIME

HOW MANY STARS?

☆ ☆ ☆ ☆ ☆

___ OUT OF FIVE

MANDATORY DAD CLICHÉ · NO. 2

TALK AT A NORMAL VOLUME UNTIL YOU ENTER A QUIET RESTAURANT. NOW EVALUATE THE MENU AT THE TOP OF YOUR LUNGS.

SIGNED WITNESS

COMPLETED SUCCESSFULLY ☐

YET TO DO ☐

CERTIFIED EXPERT ☐

NOW GIVE IT A REVIEW

☐ HIGHLY RECOMMENDED

☐ IT WAS ENJOYABLE

☐ NOT WORTH THE TIME

HOW MANY STARS?

☆ ☆ ☆ ☆ ☆

___ OUT OF FIVE

ACCIDENTALLY (AND REPEATEDLY) CALL ONE KID BY ANOTHER KID'S NAME WITHOUT ACKNOWLEDGING IT.

- [ ] COMPLETED SUCCESSFULLY
- [ ] YET TO DO
- [ ] CERTIFIED EXPERT

SIGNED WITNESS

WITNESS REENACTMENT (SKETCH)

NOW GIVE IT A REVIEW

HOW MANY STARS?

☆ ☆ ☆ ☆ ☆

___ OUT OF FIVE

- [ ] HIGHLY RECOMMENDED
- [ ] IT WAS ENJOYABLE
- [ ] NOT WORTH THE TIME

MANDATORY DAD CLICHÉ · NO. 4

IMMEDIATELY CHANGE THE FONT
SIZE ON YOUR PHONE TO THE LARGEST
POSSIBLE SETTING.

	COMPLETED SUCCESSFULLY ☐
	YET TO DO ☐
SIGNED WITNESS	CERTIFIED EXPERT ☐

MANDATORY DAD CLICHÉ · NO. 5

GOING OUT TO DINNER? TUCK THAT POLO
SHIRT INTO YOUR JEANS AND CLASS THE
ENSEMBLE UP WITH A BELT.

	COMPLETED SUCCESSFULLY ☐
	YET TO DO ☐
SIGNED WITNESS	CERTIFIED EXPERT ☐

MANDATORY DAD CLICHÉ · NO. 6

DRIVE SLOWLY IN THE FAST LANE UNTIL
SOMEONE TRIES TO PASS YOU—THEN START
RACING THEM.

	COMPLETED SUCCESSFULLY ☐
	YET TO DO ☐
SIGNED WITNESS	CERTIFIED EXPERT ☐

MANDATORY DAD CLICHÉ • NO. 7

REFUSE TO PULL OVER AND ASK FOR DIRECTIONS DESPITE HAVING ABSOLUTELY NO IDEA WHERE YOU ARE.

☐ COMPLETED SUCCESSFULLY

☐ YET TO DO

☐ CERTIFIED EXPERT

SIGNED WITNESS

NOW GIVE IT A REVIEW

HOW MANY STARS?

☆ ☆ ☆ ☆ ☆

___ OUT OF FIVE

HIGHLY RECOMMENDED ☐

IT WAS ENJOYABLE ☐

NOT WORTH THE TIME ☐

MANDATORY DAD CLICHÉ • NO. 8

FALL ASLEEP IN THE MIDDLE OF A CONVERSATION. WAKE UP & CLAIM THAT YOU DIDN'T FALL ASLEEP. FALL ASLEEP AGAIN.

☐ COMPLETED SUCCESSFULLY

☐ YET TO DO

☐ CERTIFIED EXPERT

SIGNED WITNESS

NOW GIVE IT A REVIEW

HOW MANY STARS?

☆ ☆ ☆ ☆ ☆

___ OUT OF FIVE

HIGHLY RECOMMENDED ☐

IT WAS ENJOYABLE ☐

NOT WORTH THE TIME ☐

LOUDLY SHOUT 'I'M NOT YELLING!' WHEN YOUR FAMILY ASKS YOU TO STOP YELLING.

SIGNED WITNESS

COMPLETED SUCCESSFULLY ☐

YET TO DO ☐

CERTIFIED EXPERT ☐

WITNESS REENACTMENT (SKETCH)

NOW GIVE IT A REVIEW

☐ HIGHLY RECOMMENDED

☐ IT WAS ENJOYABLE

☐ NOT WORTH THE TIME

HOW MANY STARS?

☆ ☆ ☆ ☆ ☆

___ OUT OF FIVE

GIVE YOUR CHILD A QUARTER AND TELL THEM NOT TO SPEND IT ALL IN ONE PLACE.

☐ COMPLETED SUCCESSFULLY

☐ YET TO DO

☐ CERTIFIED EXPERT

SIGNED WITNESS

WITNESS REENACTMENT (SKETCH)

NOW GIVE IT A REVIEW

HOW MANY STARS?

☆☆☆☆☆

___ OUT OF FIVE

HIGHLY RECOMMENDED ☐

IT WAS ENJOYABLE ☐

NOT WORTH THE TIME ☐

MAKE SMALL TALK WITH A CASHIER THAT IS CLEARLY NOT INTERESTED IN MAKING SMALL TALK.

SIGNED WITNESS

COMPLETED SUCCESSFULLY ☐

YET TO DO ☐

CERTIFIED EXPERT ☐

NOW GIVE IT A REVIEW

☐ HIGHLY RECOMMENDED

☐ IT WAS ENJOYABLE

☐ NOT WORTH THE TIME

HOW MANY STARS?

☆ ☆ ☆ ☆ ☆

___ OUT OF FIVE

PLAY CATCH IN THE BACKYARD AND PRETEND THAT THE BALL HURT YOUR HAND WHEN YOU CATCH IT.

SIGNED WITNESS

COMPLETED SUCCESSFULLY ☐

YET TO DO ☐

CERTIFIED EXPERT ☐

NOW GIVE IT A REVIEW

☐ HIGHLY RECOMMENDED

☐ IT WAS ENJOYABLE

☐ NOT WORTH THE TIME

HOW MANY STARS?

☆ ☆ ☆ ☆ ☆

___ OUT OF FIVE

MANDATORY DAD CLICHÉ · NO. 13

SAY 'SEE YOU NEXT YEAR!' TO EVERYONE YOU TALK TO ON NEW YEAR'S EVE.

☐ COMPLETED SUCCESSFULLY

☐ YET TO DO

☐ CERTIFIED EXPERT

SIGNED WITNESS

MANDATORY DAD CLICHÉ · NO. 14

ENCOURAGE YOUR KIDS TO FOLLOW THEIR DREAMS, BUT MUTTER 'AS LONG AS IT MAKES MONEY' UNDER YOUR BREATH.

☐ COMPLETED SUCCESSFULLY

☐ YET TO DO

☐ CERTIFIED EXPERT

SIGNED WITNESS

MANDATORY DAD CLICHÉ · NO. 15

EXCLUSIVELY WEAR BLACK SOCKS WITH SANDALS FOR AN ENTIRE BEACH VACATION.

☐ COMPLETED SUCCESSFULLY

☐ YET TO DO

☐ CERTIFIED EXPERT

SIGNED WITNESS

WHEN DECIDING TO MAKE A LARGE PURCHASE, SAY 'LET ME ASK THE BOSS' & POINT TO YOUR SIGNIFICANT OTHER.

SIGNED WITNESS

COMPLETED SUCCESSFULLY ☐

YET TO DO ☐

CERTIFIED EXPERT ☐

WITNESS REENACTMENT (SKETCH)

NOW GIVE IT A REVIEW

☐ HIGHLY RECOMMENDED

☐ IT WAS ENJOYABLE

☐ NOT WORTH THE TIME

HOW MANY STARS?

☆ ☆ ☆ ☆ ☆

____ OUT OF FIVE

WHEN SOMEONE SAYS THAT THEY ARE GOING TO GET A HAIRCUT, SAY 'YOU SHOULD GET THEM ALL CUT.'

- ☐ COMPLETED SUCCESSFULLY
- ☐ YET TO DO
- ☐ CERTIFIED EXPERT

SIGNED WITNESS

WITNESS REENACTMENT (SKETCH)

NOW GIVE IT A REVIEW

HOW MANY STARS?

☆ ☆ ☆ ☆ ☆

— OUT OF FIVE

HIGHLY RECOMMENDED ☐

IT WAS ENJOYABLE ☐

NOT WORTH THE TIME ☐

PUNISH YOUR KID FOR SAYING THE SAME WORD THAT THEY HEARD YOU SAY AT LEAST 20 TIMES YESTERDAY.

SIGNED WITNESS

COMPLETED SUCCESSFULLY ☐

YET TO DO ☐

CERTIFIED EXPERT ☐

NOW GIVE IT A REVIEW

☐ HIGHLY RECOMMENDED

☐ IT WAS ENJOYABLE

☐ NOT WORTH THE TIME

HOW MANY STARS?

☆ ☆ ☆ ☆ ☆

___ OUT OF FIVE

GET A LANYARD FOR YOUR FAVORITE PAIR OF SUNGLASSES AND WEAR THEM AROUND YOUR NECK. PREFERABLY IN NEON.

SIGNED WITNESS

COMPLETED SUCCESSFULLY ☐

YET TO DO ☐

CERTIFIED EXPERT ☐

NOW GIVE IT A REVIEW

☐ HIGHLY RECOMMENDED

☐ IT WAS ENJOYABLE

☐ NOT WORTH THE TIME

HOW MANY STARS?

☆ ☆ ☆ ☆ ☆

___ OUT OF FIVE

GRADUALLY START WEARING SHORTER AND SHORTER PANTS UNTIL THERE IS AT LEAST 3" OF YOUR LEG VISIBLE ABOVE YOUR ANKLE.

[ ] COMPLETED SUCCESSFULLY

[ ] YET TO DO

[ ] CERTIFIED EXPERT

SIGNED WITNESS

WITNESS REENACTMENT (SKETCH)

NOW GIVE IT A REVIEW

HOW MANY STARS?

☆☆☆☆☆

—— OUT OF FIVE

HIGHLY RECOMMENDED [ ]

IT WAS ENJOYABLE [ ]

NOT WORTH THE TIME [ ]

HAVE A SECRET PLACE TO STASH YOUR MONEY THAT EVERY SINGLE MEMBER OF THE FAMILY KNOWS THE LOCATION OF.

SIGNED WITNESS

COMPLETED SUCCESSFULLY ☐

YET TO DO ☐

CERTIFIED EXPERT ☐

YELL INCOHERENT WORDS SUPER-LOUDLY EVERY TIME YOU SNEEZE.

SIGNED WITNESS

COMPLETED SUCCESSFULLY ☐

YET TO DO ☐

CERTIFIED EXPERT ☐

TAKE SOME HALLOWEEN CANDY FROM YOUR KID'S BAG, SHRUG, AND SAY 'TAXES—BETTER GET USED TO IT.'

SIGNED WITNESS

COMPLETED SUCCESSFULLY ☐

YET TO DO ☐

CERTIFIED EXPERT ☐

MANDATORY DAD CLICHÉ • NO. 24

SAY 'STOP ME IF I'VE TOLD YOU THIS BEFORE' AND CONTINUE TELLING THE SAME STORY THAT YOU'VE TOLD 50 TIMES.

☐ COMPLETED SUCCESSFULLY

☐ YET TO DO

☐ CERTIFIED EXPERT

SIGNED WITNESS

NOW GIVE IT A REVIEW

HOW MANY STARS?

☆ ☆ ☆ ☆ ☆

___ OUT OF FIVE

HIGHLY RECOMMENDED ☐

IT WAS ENJOYABLE ☐

NOT WORTH THE TIME ☐

MANDATORY DAD CLICHÉ • NO. 25

AT A DIMLY-LIT ROMANTIC RESTAURANT? BETTER TURN YOUR PHONE LIGHT ON FULL BRIGHTNESS TO READ THE MENU.

☐ COMPLETED SUCCESSFULLY

☐ YET TO DO

☐ CERTIFIED EXPERT

SIGNED WITNESS

NOW GIVE IT A REVIEW

HOW MANY STARS?

☆ ☆ ☆ ☆ ☆

___ OUT OF FIVE

HIGHLY RECOMMENDED ☐

IT WAS ENJOYABLE ☐

NOT WORTH THE TIME ☐

MANDATORY DAD CLICHÉ · NO. 26

HAVE YOUR OWN 'SPECIAL SAUCE' THAT IS OBVIOUSLY JUST KETCHUP AND MUSTARD MIXED TOGETHER.

SIGNED WITNESS

COMPLETED SUCCESSFULLY ☐

YET TO DO ☐

CERTIFIED EXPERT ☐

NOW GIVE IT A REVIEW

☐ HIGHLY RECOMMENDED

☐ IT WAS ENJOYABLE

☐ NOT WORTH THE TIME

HOW MANY STARS?

☆ ☆ ☆ ☆ ☆

___ OUT OF FIVE

MANDATORY DAD CLICHÉ · NO. 27

YELL THAT YOUR KIDS 'SHOULD HAVE GONE BEFORE WE LEFT' WHEN THEY NEED TO USE THE RESTROOM 5 HOURS INTO A ROAD TRIP.

SIGNED WITNESS

COMPLETED SUCCESSFULLY ☐

YET TO DO ☐

CERTIFIED EXPERT ☐

NOW GIVE IT A REVIEW

☐ HIGHLY RECOMMENDED

☐ IT WAS ENJOYABLE

☐ NOT WORTH THE TIME

HOW MANY STARS?

☆ ☆ ☆ ☆ ☆

___ OUT OF FIVE

HAVE A FEW BEERS WITH THE GUYS. BE SURE TO REST YOUR HANDS HIGHER AND HIGHER ON YOUR HIPS AFTER EVERY ROUND.

☐ COMPLETED SUCCESSFULLY

☐ YET TO DO

☐ CERTIFIED EXPERT

SIGNED WITNESS

WITNESS REENACTMENT (SKETCH)

NOW GIVE IT A REVIEW

HOW MANY STARS?

☆ ☆ ☆ ☆ ☆

— OUT OF FIVE

HIGHLY RECOMMENDED ☐

IT WAS ENJOYABLE ☐

NOT WORTH THE TIME ☐

TELL PEOPLE ABOUT SOMETHING YOU SAW ON THE FACEBOOK, RIGHT BEFORE ORDERING SOMETHING ON THE AMAZON.

SIGNED WITNESS

COMPLETED SUCCESSFULLY ☐

YET TO DO ☐

CERTIFIED EXPERT ☐

WITNESS REENACTMENT (SKETCH)

NOW GIVE IT A REVIEW

☐ HIGHLY RECOMMENDED

☐ IT WAS ENJOYABLE

☐ NOT WORTH THE TIME

HOW MANY STARS?

☆ ☆ ☆ ☆ ☆

___ OUT OF FIVE

MANDATORY DAD CLICHÉ • NO. 30

RECKLESSLY DRIVE YOUR FAMILY AT 90 MPH TO THE MOVIES SO AS NOT TO RISK MISSING THE TRAILERS.

☐ COMPLETED SUCCESSFULLY

☐ YET TO DO

☐ CERTIFIED EXPERT

SIGNED WITNESS

MANDATORY DAD CLICHÉ • NO. 31

FINALLY BUY THAT PAIR OF BLINDINGLY-WHITE NEW BALANCES THAT YOU'VE HAD YOUR EYE ON.

☐ COMPLETED SUCCESSFULLY

☐ YET TO DO

☐ CERTIFIED EXPERT

SIGNED WITNESS

MANDATORY DAD CLICHÉ • NO. 32

SOMEHOW ALWAYS WALK DOWN STAIRS LOUDER THAN WHAT SEEMS HUMANLY POSSIBLE.

☐ COMPLETED SUCCESSFULLY

☐ YET TO DO

☐ CERTIFIED EXPERT

SIGNED WITNESS

WHEN THE CHECK COMES AT A RESTAURANT, PUT ON SOME BIFOCALS AS YOU SQUINT AND SAY 'LET'S SEE WHAT THE DAMAGE IS.'

SIGNED WITNESS

COMPLETED SUCCESSFULLY ☐

YET TO DO ☐

CERTIFIED EXPERT ☐

WITNESS REENACTMENT (SKETCH)

NOW GIVE IT A REVIEW

☐ HIGHLY RECOMMENDED

☐ IT WAS ENJOYABLE

☐ NOT WORTH THE TIME

HOW MANY STARS?

☆☆☆☆☆

___ OUT OF FIVE

SET THE GPS FOR YOUR DESTINATION, SEE THE ESTIMATED ARRIVAL TIME, AND TAKE IT AS A WORLD RECORD TO TRY AND BEAT.

- [ ] COMPLETED SUCCESSFULLY
- [ ] YET TO DO
- [ ] CERTIFIED EXPERT

SIGNED WITNESS

WITNESS REENACTMENT (SKETCH)

NOW GIVE IT A REVIEW

HOW MANY STARS?

☆☆☆☆☆

— OUT OF FIVE

- [ ] HIGHLY RECOMMENDED
- [ ] IT WAS ENJOYABLE
- [ ] NOT WORTH THE TIME

MANDATORY DAD CLICHÉ · NO. 35

START A NEW PROJECT AROUND THE HOUSE, THEN IMMEDIATELY SPEND 25 MINUTES LOOKING FOR THE TAPE MEASURE YOU JUST HAD.

SIGNED WITNESS

COMPLETED SUCCESSFULLY ☐

YET TO DO ☐

CERTIFIED EXPERT ☐

NOW GIVE IT A REVIEW

☐ HIGHLY RECOMMENDED

☐ IT WAS ENJOYABLE

☐ NOT WORTH THE TIME

HOW MANY STARS?

☆☆☆☆☆

___ OUT OF FIVE

MANDATORY DAD CLICHÉ · NO. 36

SHAKE HANDFULS OF M&M'S IN YOUR HAND LIKE YOU'RE PLAYING CRAPS BEFORE TOSSING THEM IN YOUR MOUTH.

SIGNED WITNESS

COMPLETED SUCCESSFULLY ☐

YET TO DO ☐

CERTIFIED EXPERT ☐

NOW GIVE IT A REVIEW

☐ HIGHLY RECOMMENDED

☐ IT WAS ENJOYABLE

☐ NOT WORTH THE TIME

HOW MANY STARS?

☆☆☆☆☆

___ OUT OF FIVE

BEHIND SOMEONE AT A RED LIGHT? HONK AT THE CAR IN FRONT OF YOU .2 SECONDS AFTER THE LIGHT CHANGES.

☐ COMPLETED SUCCESSFULLY

☐ YET TO DO

☐ CERTIFIED EXPERT

SIGNED WITNESS

NOW GIVE IT A REVIEW

HOW MANY STARS?

☆ ☆ ☆ ☆ ☆

____ OUT OF FIVE

HIGHLY RECOMMENDED ☐

IT WAS ENJOYABLE ☐

NOT WORTH THE TIME ☐

FIRST CAR AT A RED LIGHT? STARE INTO THE DISTANCE AS IT TURNS GREEN & THEN YELLOW. PULL THROUGH AS IT TURNS RED AGAIN.

☐ COMPLETED SUCCESSFULLY

☐ YET TO DO

☐ CERTIFIED EXPERT

SIGNED WITNESS

NOW GIVE IT A REVIEW

HOW MANY STARS?

☆ ☆ ☆ ☆ ☆

____ OUT OF FIVE

HIGHLY RECOMMENDED ☐

IT WAS ENJOYABLE ☐

NOT WORTH THE TIME ☐

MANDATORY DAD CLICHÉ · NO. 39

KEEP EVERY SINGLE RECEIPT IN YOUR WALLET. BOUGHT A DONUT TWO MONTHS AGO? BETTER SAVE IT—JUST IN CASE.

SIGNED WITNESS

COMPLETED SUCCESSFULLY ☐

YET TO DO ☐

CERTIFIED EXPERT ☐

WITNESS REENACTMENT (SKETCH)

NOW GIVE IT A REVIEW

☐ HIGHLY RECOMMENDED

☐ IT WAS ENJOYABLE

☐ NOT WORTH THE TIME

HOW MANY STARS?

☆☆☆☆☆

___ OUT OF FIVE

SUDDENLY DECIDE TO START BACKING INTO EVERY PARKING SPOT. ALSO, HAVE NO CLEAR EXPLANATION AS TO WHY.

☐ COMPLETED SUCCESSFULLY

☐ YET TO DO

☐ CERTIFIED EXPERT

SIGNED WITNESS

WITNESS REENACTMENT (SKETCH)

NOW GIVE IT A REVIEW

HOW MANY STARS?

☆ ☆ ☆ ☆ ☆

— OUT OF FIVE

HIGHLY RECOMMENDED ☐

IT WAS ENJOYABLE ☐

NOT WORTH THE TIME ☐

IF YOUR KID OPENS UP CANDY IN THE BACK WHILE YOU'RE DRIVING, SILENTLY REACH YOUR HAND BACKWARDS UNTIL THEY GIVE YOU SOME.

COMPLETED SUCCESSFULLY ☐

YET TO DO ☐

SIGNED WITNESS

CERTIFIED EXPERT ☐

KEEP YOUR CELL PHONE AT HOME, NO WHERE NEAR YOU, PLUGGED INTO AN OUTLET 24/7–IN CASE OF EMERGENCIES.

COMPLETED SUCCESSFULLY ☐

YET TO DO ☐

SIGNED WITNESS

CERTIFIED EXPERT ☐

LAUGH TO YOURSELF AT SOMETHING INAPPROPRIATE THAT YOU JUST SAID–AND THEN SAY 'THAT'S NOT FUNNY.'

COMPLETED SUCCESSFULLY ☐

YET TO DO ☐

SIGNED WITNESS

CERTIFIED EXPERT ☐

MANDATORY DAD CLICHÉ · NO. 44

FOR ONE WEEK, GET UP AT DAWN AND EXERCISE. TALK NON-STOP ABOUT HOW GOOD IT FEELS. NOW NEVER DO IT AGAIN.

☐ COMPLETED SUCCESSFULLY

☐ YET TO DO

☐ CERTIFIED EXPERT

SIGNED WITNESS

NOW GIVE IT A REVIEW

HOW MANY STARS?

☆ ☆ ☆ ☆ ☆

___ OUT OF FIVE

HIGHLY RECOMMENDED ☐

IT WAS ENJOYABLE ☐

NOT WORTH THE TIME ☐

MANDATORY DAD CLICHÉ · NO. 45

SAY THINGS LIKE 'WERE YOU RAISED IN A BARN?' WHEN, IN FACT, YOU WERE THE ONE THAT RAISED THEM.

☐ COMPLETED SUCCESSFULLY

☐ YET TO DO

☐ CERTIFIED EXPERT

SIGNED WITNESS

NOW GIVE IT A REVIEW

HOW MANY STARS?

☆ ☆ ☆ ☆ ☆

___ OUT OF FIVE

HIGHLY RECOMMENDED ☐

IT WAS ENJOYABLE ☐

NOT WORTH THE TIME ☐

KEEP THE CABLES & POWER CORDS FOR EVERY ELECTRONIC DEVICE YOU HAVE EVER OWNED IN A CARDBOARD BOX IN THE BASEMENT—TANGLED.

SIGNED WITNESS

COMPLETED SUCCESSFULLY ☐

YET TO DO ☐

CERTIFIED EXPERT ☐

WITNESS REENACTMENT (SKETCH)

NOW GIVE IT A REVIEW

☐ HIGHLY RECOMMENDED

☐ IT WAS ENJOYABLE

☐ NOT WORTH THE TIME

HOW MANY STARS?

☆☆☆☆☆

____ OUT OF FIVE

MANDATORY DAD CLICHÉ • NO. 47

GIVE YOUR KIDS A LECTURE THAT 'MONEY DOESN'T GROW ON TREES' WHILE ORDERING THREE APPETIZERS AT APPLEBEE'S.

☐ COMPLETED SUCCESSFULLY

☐ YET TO DO

☐ CERTIFIED EXPERT

SIGNED WITNESS

WITNESS REENACTMENT (SKETCH)

NOW GIVE IT A REVIEW

HOW MANY STARS?

☆☆☆☆☆

—— OUT OF FIVE

HIGHLY RECOMMENDED ☐

IT WAS ENJOYABLE ☐

NOT WORTH THE TIME ☐

ANSWER AN INCOMING PHONE CALL FROM SOMEONE THAT YOU KNOW WITH A HARDY 'YELLO!'

SIGNED WITNESS

COMPLETED SUCCESSFULLY ☐

YET TO DO ☐

CERTIFIED EXPERT ☐

NOW GIVE IT A REVIEW

☐ HIGHLY RECOMMENDED

☐ IT WAS ENJOYABLE

☐ NOT WORTH THE TIME

HOW MANY STARS?

☆☆☆☆☆

___ OUT OF FIVE

TRY TO THROW GARBAGE INTO THE TRASH CAN INSTEAD OF WALKING TWO MORE FEET. IF YOU HAPPEN TO MAKE IT, YELL '3 POINTS!'

SIGNED WITNESS

COMPLETED SUCCESSFULLY ☐

YET TO DO ☐

CERTIFIED EXPERT ☐

NOW GIVE IT A REVIEW

☐ HIGHLY RECOMMENDED

☐ IT WAS ENJOYABLE

☐ NOT WORTH THE TIME

HOW MANY STARS?

☆☆☆☆☆

___ OUT OF FIVE

SUDDENLY CARE WAY TOO MUCH ABOUT YOUR LAWN—BUT JUST WALK AROUND IT, LOOKING AT IT FROM DIFFERENT ANGLES FOR HOURS.

- [ ] COMPLETED SUCCESSFULLY
- [ ] YET TO DO
- [ ] CERTIFIED EXPERT

SIGNED WITNESS

WITNESS REENACTMENT (SKETCH)

NOW GIVE IT A REVIEW

HOW MANY STARS?

☆☆☆☆☆

—— OUT OF FIVE

HIGHLY RECOMMENDED [ ]

IT WAS ENJOYABLE [ ]

NOT WORTH THE TIME [ ]

EXCLUSIVELY ANSWER ALL 'WHY DOES...' QUESTIONS WITH THE SINGLE WORD 'BECAUSE.'

COMPLETED SUCCESSFULLY ☐

YET TO DO ☐

CERTIFIED EXPERT ☐

SIGNED WITNESS

NOW GIVE IT A REVIEW

☐ HIGHLY RECOMMENDED

☐ IT WAS ENJOYABLE

☐ NOT WORTH THE TIME

HOW MANY STARS?

☆ ☆ ☆ ☆ ☆

___ OUT OF FIVE

GET UNREASONABLY MAD WHILE PLAYING SCRABBLE WITH YOUR FAMILY. BONUS: INCLUDE A RANT ABOUT TWO LETTER WORDS.

COMPLETED SUCCESSFULLY ☐

YET TO DO ☐

CERTIFIED EXPERT ☐

SIGNED WITNESS

NOW GIVE IT A REVIEW

☐ HIGHLY RECOMMENDED

☐ IT WAS ENJOYABLE

☐ NOT WORTH THE TIME

HOW MANY STARS?

☆ ☆ ☆ ☆ ☆

___ OUT OF FIVE

APPROACHING A MODERATELY BUSY INTERSECTION WHILE DRIVING? BETTER TURN OFF THAT RADIO.

☐ COMPLETED SUCCESSFULLY

☐ YET TO DO

☐ CERTIFIED EXPERT

SIGNED WITNESS

NOW GIVE IT A REVIEW

HOW MANY STARS?

☆ ☆ ☆ ☆ ☆

___ OUT OF FIVE

HIGHLY RECOMMENDED ☐

IT WAS ENJOYABLE ☐

NOT WORTH THE TIME ☐

SERVE CLEARLY POISONOUS FOOD WHILE SAYING SOMETHING LIKE 'JUST EAT AROUND THE BAD PARTS, IT'S STILL GOOD.'

☐ COMPLETED SUCCESSFULLY

☐ YET TO DO

☐ CERTIFIED EXPERT

SIGNED WITNESS

NOW GIVE IT A REVIEW

HOW MANY STARS?

☆ ☆ ☆ ☆ ☆

___ OUT OF FIVE

HIGHLY RECOMMENDED ☐

IT WAS ENJOYABLE ☐

NOT WORTH THE TIME ☐

COMPLAIN ABOUT HOW MUSIC THESE DAYS IS ALL NONSENSE, BEFORE PLAYING A REAL CLASSIC LIKE 'SUSSUDIO.'

	COMPLETED SUCCESSFULLY ☐
	YET TO DO ☐
SIGNED WITNESS	CERTIFIED EXPERT ☐

WITNESS REENACTMENT (SKETCH)

NOW GIVE IT A REVIEW

☐ HIGHLY RECOMMENDED

☐ IT WAS ENJOYABLE

☐ NOT WORTH THE TIME

HOW MANY STARS?

☆☆☆☆☆

___ OUT OF FIVE

PRESSURE WASH YOUR FENCE. AND YOUR DECK. AND YOUR DRIVEWAY. AND YOUR SIDING. AND LITERALLY ANYTHING ELSE YOU CAN FIND.

☐ COMPLETED SUCCESSFULLY

☐ YET TO DO

☐ CERTIFIED EXPERT

SIGNED WITNESS

WITNESS REENACTMENT (SKETCH)

NOW GIVE IT A REVIEW

HOW MANY STARS?

☆ ☆ ☆ ☆ ☆

___ OUT OF FIVE

HIGHLY RECOMMENDED ☐

IT WAS ENJOYABLE ☐

NOT WORTH THE TIME ☐

PRIMARILY FILL YOUR WARDROBE WITH T-SHIRTS YOU BUY ON VACATION—ONES THAT JUST SAY 'PALM BEACH' OR SOMETHING.

SIGNED WITNESS

COMPLETED SUCCESSFULLY ☐

YET TO DO ☐

CERTIFIED EXPERT ☐

NOW GIVE IT A REVIEW

☐ HIGHLY RECOMMENDED

☐ IT WAS ENJOYABLE

☐ NOT WORTH THE TIME

HOW MANY STARS?

☆☆☆☆☆

___ OUT OF FIVE

WHEN YOU'RE ASKED HOW YOU DID SOMETHING, SIMPLY RESPOND 'MAGIC.' GETS THEM EVERY TIME.

SIGNED WITNESS

COMPLETED SUCCESSFULLY ☐

YET TO DO ☐

CERTIFIED EXPERT ☐

NOW GIVE IT A REVIEW

☐ HIGHLY RECOMMENDED

☐ IT WAS ENJOYABLE

☐ NOT WORTH THE TIME

HOW MANY STARS?

☆☆☆☆☆

___ OUT OF FIVE

MANDATORY DAD CLICHÉ • NO. 59

TEAR UP LISTENING TO 'CATS IN THE CRADLE,' BUT SPEND YOUR WEEKENDS PUTTING IN A FEW EXTRA HOURS AT WORK.

☐ COMPLETED SUCCESSFULLY

☐ YET TO DO

☐ CERTIFIED EXPERT

SIGNED WITNESS

MANDATORY DAD CLICHÉ • NO. 60

TAKE OFF YOUR SOCKS IN RANDOM LOCATIONS THROUGHOUT THE HOUSE. NOT IN PAIRS EITHER. SINGLES. REALLY KEEP THEM GUESSING.

☐ COMPLETED SUCCESSFULLY

☐ YET TO DO

☐ CERTIFIED EXPERT

SIGNED WITNESS

MANDATORY DAD CLICHÉ • NO. 61

INSIST THAT YOUR GROWN KIDS KEEP JUMPER CABLES IN THEIR CARS—BUT NEVER BOTHER TO EXPLAIN HOW TO ACTUALLY USE THEM.

☐ COMPLETED SUCCESSFULLY

☐ YET TO DO

☐ CERTIFIED EXPERT

SIGNED WITNESS

WASTE 2 FULL DAYS TRYING TO REPAIR SOMETHING INSTEAD OF SPENDING FIFTEEN DOLLARS TO REPLACE IT.

SIGNED WITNESS

COMPLETED SUCCESSFULLY ☐

YET TO DO ☐

CERTIFIED EXPERT ☐

WITNESS REENACTMENT (SKETCH)

NOW GIVE IT A REVIEW

☐ HIGHLY RECOMMENDED

☐ IT WAS ENJOYABLE

☐ NOT WORTH THE TIME

HOW MANY STARS?

☆ ☆ ☆ ☆ ☆

___ OUT OF FIVE

PRETEND TO KNOW WHAT'S WRONG WITH AN APPLIANCE—BUT COMPLAIN THAT 'THEY MAKE IT SO YOU CAN'T WORK ON THEM ANYMORE.'

☐ COMPLETED SUCCESSFULLY

☐ YET TO DO

☐ CERTIFIED EXPERT

SIGNED WITNESS

WITNESS REENACTMENT (SKETCH)

NOW GIVE IT A REVIEW

HOW MANY STARS?

☆☆☆☆☆

—— OUT OF FIVE

HIGHLY RECOMMENDED ☐

IT WAS ENJOYABLE ☐

NOT WORTH THE TIME ☐

RUIN ALL MOVIES BY LOUDLY STATING 'THAT COULD NEVER ACTUALLY HAPPEN.' EVEN DURING THE SUPERHERO ONES.

COMPLETED SUCCESSFULLY ☐

YET TO DO ☐

CERTIFIED EXPERT ☐

SIGNED WITNESS

NOW GIVE IT A REVIEW

☐ HIGHLY RECOMMENDED

☐ IT WAS ENJOYABLE

☐ NOT WORTH THE TIME

HOW MANY STARS?

☆ ☆ ☆ ☆ ☆

____ OUT OF FIVE

SPECIAL OCCASION? PUT ON SOME PANTS THAT HAVE OBVIOUSLY NEVER BEEN WORN. BONUS POINTS IF THEY STILL HAVE A STICKER ON THEM.

COMPLETED SUCCESSFULLY ☐

YET TO DO ☐

CERTIFIED EXPERT ☐

SIGNED WITNESS

NOW GIVE IT A REVIEW

☐ HIGHLY RECOMMENDED

☐ IT WAS ENJOYABLE

☐ NOT WORTH THE TIME

HOW MANY STARS?

☆ ☆ ☆ ☆ ☆

____ OUT OF FIVE

WHEN ANYTHING EVEN REMOTELY CLOSE TO A SEX SCENE COMES ON TV, CLOSE YOUR EYES & PRETEND TO BE ASLEEP.

☐ COMPLETED SUCCESSFULLY

☐ YET TO DO

☐ CERTIFIED EXPERT

SIGNED WITNESS

WITNESS REENACTMENT (SKETCH)

NOW GIVE IT A REVIEW

HOW MANY STARS?

☆☆☆☆☆

___ OUT OF FIVE

HIGHLY RECOMMENDED ☐

IT WAS ENJOYABLE ☐

NOT WORTH THE TIME ☐

MANDATORY DAD CLICHÉ · NO. 67

HAVE PHONE CONVERSATIONS WITH YOUR KIDS THAT CONSIST SOLELY WITH 'HOW'S THE WEATHER?' AND 'HERE'S YOUR MOTHER.'

SIGNED WITNESS

COMPLETED SUCCESSFULLY ☐

YET TO DO ☐

CERTIFIED EXPERT ☐

MANDATORY DAD CLICHÉ · NO. 68

ATTEMPT TO REPLACE A DEAD FISH W/ A NEW ONE BEFORE ANYONE NOTICES. ALSO, WISH YOU HAD PAID ATTENTION TO WHAT COLOR IT WAS.

SIGNED WITNESS

COMPLETED SUCCESSFULLY ☐

YET TO DO ☐

CERTIFIED EXPERT ☐

MANDATORY DAD CLICHÉ · NO. 69

KEEP NO LESS THAN 30 PAIRS OF JEANS IN YOUR CLOSET, BUT ONLY WEAR THE SAME PAIR OVER AND OVER.

SIGNED WITNESS

COMPLETED SUCCESSFULLY ☐

YET TO DO ☐

CERTIFIED EXPERT ☐

REMIND YOUR KID EVERY SINGLE YEAR FOR THE REST OF YOUR LIFE ABOUT THE TIME THEY WERE 7 & POOPED THEIR PANTS ON VACATION.

- [ ] COMPLETED SUCCESSFULLY
- [ ] YET TO DO
- [ ] CERTIFIED EXPERT

SIGNED WITNESS

NOW GIVE IT A REVIEW

HOW MANY STARS?
☆☆☆☆☆
___ OUT OF FIVE

HIGHLY RECOMMENDED [ ]

IT WAS ENJOYABLE [ ]

NOT WORTH THE TIME [ ]

TEACH YOUR CHILDREN THAT WINNING ISN'T IMPORTANT—APPARENTLY BY FLIPPING OVER THE MONOPOLY BOARD WHEN YOU'RE BANKRUPT.

- [ ] COMPLETED SUCCESSFULLY
- [ ] YET TO DO
- [ ] CERTIFIED EXPERT

SIGNED WITNESS

NOW GIVE IT A REVIEW

HOW MANY STARS?
☆☆☆☆☆
___ OUT OF FIVE

HIGHLY RECOMMENDED [ ]

IT WAS ENJOYABLE [ ]

NOT WORTH THE TIME [ ]

WHEN YOUR CAR BREAKS DOWN, OPEN UP THE HOOD AND STARE AT IT FOR A GOOD LONG WHILE BEFORE CALLING A MECHANIC.

SIGNED WITNESS

COMPLETED SUCCESSFULLY ☐

YET TO DO ☐

CERTIFIED EXPERT ☐

NOW GIVE IT A REVIEW

☐ HIGHLY RECOMMENDED

☐ IT WAS ENJOYABLE

☐ NOT WORTH THE TIME

HOW MANY STARS?

☆ ☆ ☆ ☆ ☆

___ OUT OF FIVE

NOD ALONG AND SAY 'YEAH THAT'S WHAT I THOUGHT' NO MATTER WHAT THE MECHANIC TELLS YOU IS WRONG WITH YOUR CAR.

SIGNED WITNESS

COMPLETED SUCCESSFULLY ☐

YET TO DO ☐

CERTIFIED EXPERT ☐

NOW GIVE IT A REVIEW

☐ HIGHLY RECOMMENDED

☐ IT WAS ENJOYABLE

☐ NOT WORTH THE TIME

HOW MANY STARS?

☆ ☆ ☆ ☆ ☆

___ OUT OF FIVE

TELL YOUR KIDS THAT 'A LITTLE HARD WORK
NEVER HURT ANYBODY' WHILE DRINKING ICED
TEA & WATCHING THEM MOW THE LAWN.

☐ COMPLETED SUCCESSFULLY

☐ YET TO DO

☐ CERTIFIED EXPERT

SIGNED WITNESS

WITNESS REENACTMENT (SKETCH)

NOW GIVE IT A REVIEW

HOW MANY STARS?

☆ ☆ ☆ ☆ ☆

___ OUT OF FIVE

HIGHLY RECOMMENDED ☐

IT WAS ENJOYABLE ☐

NOT WORTH THE TIME ☐

TAKE THOUSANDS OF PHOTOS DURING THE FIRST FIVE YEARS OF YOUR CHILD'S LIFE, AND THEN ONE FOR EVERY YEAR AFTER THAT.

SIGNED WITNESS

COMPLETED SUCCESSFULLY ☐

YET TO DO ☐

CERTIFIED EXPERT ☐

WITNESS REENACTMENT (SKETCH)

NOW GIVE IT A REVIEW

☐ HIGHLY RECOMMENDED

☐ IT WAS ENJOYABLE

☐ NOT WORTH THE TIME

HOW MANY STARS?

☆☆☆☆☆

___ OUT OF FIVE

MANDATORY DAD CLICHÉ · NO. 76

THROW YOUR KIDS REALLY HIGH UP IN THE AIR AND CATCH THEM—UNTIL A MORE RESPONSIBLE INDIVIDUAL TELLS YOU TO STOP.

- [ ] COMPLETED SUCCESSFULLY
- [ ] YET TO DO
- [ ] CERTIFIED EXPERT

SIGNED WITNESS

MANDATORY DAD CLICHÉ · NO. 77

BUY NEW EXERCISE EQUIPMENT & USE IT RELIGIOUSLY FOR A MONTH. CONTINUE USING IT AFTER THAT—JUST NOW TO HOLD CLOTHES.

- [ ] COMPLETED SUCCESSFULLY
- [ ] YET TO DO
- [ ] CERTIFIED EXPERT

SIGNED WITNESS

MANDATORY DAD CLICHÉ · NO. 78

READ YOUR KID A BEDTIME STORY, BUT MAKE UP YOUR OWN ENDING ABOUT 10 PAGES EARLY BECAUSE, SERIOUSLY, GO TO SLEEP ALREADY.

- [ ] COMPLETED SUCCESSFULLY
- [ ] YET TO DO
- [ ] CERTIFIED EXPERT

SIGNED WITNESS

WORRY THAT EVERYTHING IS A COMPUTER VIRUS—BUT DON'T LET THAT STOP YOU FROM CLICKING ON EVERY LINK IMAGINABLE.

COMPLETED SUCCESSFULLY ☐

YET TO DO ☐

CERTIFIED EXPERT ☐

SIGNED WITNESS

WITNESS REENACTMENT (SKETCH)

NOW GIVE IT A REVIEW

☐ HIGHLY RECOMMENDED

☐ IT WAS ENJOYABLE

☐ NOT WORTH THE TIME

HOW MANY STARS?

☆☆☆☆☆

___ OUT OF FIVE

PROCLAIM THAT A 'PENNY SAVED IS A PENNY EARNED' EVERY CHANCE YOU GET. SURE, SO IS A PENNY SPENT—BUT STOP BEING SO LITERAL.

- [ ] COMPLETED SUCCESSFULLY
- [ ] YET TO DO
- [ ] CERTIFIED EXPERT

SIGNED WITNESS

WITNESS REENACTMENT (SKETCH)

NOW GIVE IT A REVIEW

HOW MANY STARS?

☆ ☆ ☆ ☆ ☆

— OUT OF FIVE

- HIGHLY RECOMMENDED [ ]
- IT WAS ENJOYABLE [ ]
- NOT WORTH THE TIME [ ]

CONSTANTLY CALL THE PERSON THAT YOUR KID IS DATING BY THE WRONG NAME. BE CREATIVE. HAVE FUN WITH IT.

SIGNED WITNESS

COMPLETED SUCCESSFULLY ☐

YET TO DO ☐

CERTIFIED EXPERT ☐

NOW GIVE IT A REVIEW

☐ HIGHLY RECOMMENDED

☐ IT WAS ENJOYABLE

☐ NOT WORTH THE TIME

HOW MANY STARS?

☆ ☆ ☆ ☆ ☆

___ OUT OF FIVE

KEEP THE HOUSE AT A COMPLETELY NORMAL, NOT-INSANE-AT-ALL, 85 DEGREES IN THE SUMMERTIME.

SIGNED WITNESS

COMPLETED SUCCESSFULLY ☐

YET TO DO ☐

CERTIFIED EXPERT ☐

NOW GIVE IT A REVIEW

☐ HIGHLY RECOMMENDED

☐ IT WAS ENJOYABLE

☐ NOT WORTH THE TIME

HOW MANY STARS?

☆ ☆ ☆ ☆ ☆

___ OUT OF FIVE

SLEEP THROUGH FIVE PEOPLE SCREAMING YOUR NAME AFTER FALLING ASLEEP WATCHING A FOOTBALL GAME ON TV.

- [ ] COMPLETED SUCCESSFULLY
- [ ] YET TO DO
- [ ] CERTIFIED EXPERT

SIGNED WITNESS

NOW GIVE IT A REVIEW

HOW MANY STARS?

☆ ☆ ☆ ☆ ☆

___ OUT OF FIVE

HIGHLY RECOMMENDED [ ]

IT WAS ENJOYABLE [ ]

NOT WORTH THE TIME [ ]

INSTANTLY WAKE UP FROM A COMA-LIKE SLEEP AFTER HEARING A SINGLE FLOORBOARD CREAK 15 MINUTES PAST CURFEW.

- [ ] COMPLETED SUCCESSFULLY
- [ ] YET TO DO
- [ ] CERTIFIED EXPERT

SIGNED WITNESS

NOW GIVE IT A REVIEW

HOW MANY STARS?

☆ ☆ ☆ ☆ ☆

___ OUT OF FIVE

HIGHLY RECOMMENDED [ ]

IT WAS ENJOYABLE [ ]

NOT WORTH THE TIME [ ]

RELUCTANTLY AGREE TO ADOPT A DOG AFTER YEARS OF NON-STOP BEGGING – IMMEDIATELY LOVE IT MORE THAN YOUR OWN CHILDREN.

SIGNED WITNESS

COMPLETED SUCCESSFULLY ☐

YET TO DO ☐

CERTIFIED EXPERT ☐

WITNESS REENACTMENT (SKETCH)

NOW GIVE IT A REVIEW

☐ HIGHLY RECOMMENDED

☐ IT WAS ENJOYABLE

☐ NOT WORTH THE TIME

HOW MANY STARS?

☆☆☆☆☆

___ OUT OF FIVE

SAY SOMETHING THAT YOU ALWAYS THOUGHT WAS FUNNY—WHICH YOUR KIDS THEN INFORM YOU IS RACIST.

☐ COMPLETED SUCCESSFULLY

☐ YET TO DO

☐ CERTIFIED EXPERT

SIGNED WITNESS

WITNESS REENACTMENT (SKETCH)

NOW GIVE IT A REVIEW

HOW MANY STARS?

☆☆☆☆☆

—— OUT OF FIVE

HIGHLY RECOMMENDED ☐

IT WAS ENJOYABLE ☐

NOT WORTH THE TIME ☐

MANDATORY DAD CLICHÉ • NO. 87

RATIONALLY DEAL WITH STEPPING ON
YOUR KID'S TOY BAREFOOT BY DROP-KICKING
IT ACROSS THE ROOM.

COMPLETED SUCCESSFULLY ☐

YET TO DO ☐

CERTIFIED EXPERT ☐

SIGNED WITNESS

MANDATORY DAD CLICHÉ • NO. 88

SQUIRT APPROXIMATELY TWO GALLONS
MORE LIGHTER FLUID THAN NECESSARY TO
START UP THE GRILL.

COMPLETED SUCCESSFULLY ☐

YET TO DO ☐

CERTIFIED EXPERT ☐

SIGNED WITNESS

MANDATORY DAD CLICHÉ • NO. 89

BUY A BELT CLIP FOR YOUR PHONE, AND
FINALLY END THE NIGHTMARE OF TAKING IT
IN & OUT OF YOUR POCKET.

COMPLETED SUCCESSFULLY ☐

YET TO DO ☐

CERTIFIED EXPERT ☐

SIGNED WITNESS

MANDATORY DAD CLICHÉ • NO. 90

PUNISH YOUR KIDS FOR HAVING DRUGS & ALCOHOL IN THE HOUSE. CONFISCATE THEM. ENJOY THE DRUGS & ALCOHOL IN THE HOUSE.

- [ ] COMPLETED SUCCESSFULLY
- [ ] YET TO DO
- [ ] CERTIFIED EXPERT

SIGNED WITNESS

NOW GIVE IT A REVIEW

HOW MANY STARS?

☆ ☆ ☆ ☆ ☆

___ OUT OF FIVE

- HIGHLY RECOMMENDED [ ]
- IT WAS ENJOYABLE [ ]
- NOT WORTH THE TIME [ ]

MANDATORY DAD CLICHÉ • NO. 91

SAY THINGS LIKE 'I ONLY WANT TO MAKE YOU HAPPY' WHILE MAKING YOUR KIDS DO THINGS THAT DON'T MAKE THEM HAPPY.

- [ ] COMPLETED SUCCESSFULLY
- [ ] YET TO DO
- [ ] CERTIFIED EXPERT

SIGNED WITNESS

NOW GIVE IT A REVIEW

HOW MANY STARS?

☆ ☆ ☆ ☆ ☆

___ OUT OF FIVE

- HIGHLY RECOMMENDED [ ]
- IT WAS ENJOYABLE [ ]
- NOT WORTH THE TIME [ ]

MAKE SURE THAT YOUR CHILDREN DON'T LEAVE THE HOUSE IN ANYTHING MORE REVEALING THAN A BURLAP SACK.

SIGNED WITNESS

COMPLETED SUCCESSFULLY ☐

YET TO DO ☐

CERTIFIED EXPERT ☐

WITNESS REENACTMENT (SKETCH)

NOW GIVE IT A REVIEW

☐ HIGHLY RECOMMENDED

☐ IT WAS ENJOYABLE

☐ NOT WORTH THE TIME

HOW MANY STARS?

☆ ☆ ☆ ☆ ☆

___ OUT OF FIVE

SHARE SOME 'REAL' MUSIC WITH YOUR KIDS THAT THEY WILL INSTANTLY HATE AND BEG YOU TO TURN OFF.

☐ COMPLETED SUCCESSFULLY

☐ YET TO DO

☐ CERTIFIED EXPERT

SIGNED WITNESS

WITNESS REENACTMENT (SKETCH)

NOW GIVE IT A REVIEW

HOW MANY STARS?

☆ ☆ ☆ ☆ ☆

___ OUT OF FIVE

HIGHLY RECOMMENDED ☐

IT WAS ENJOYABLE ☐

NOT WORTH THE TIME ☐

ACT LIKE A TOUR GUIDE WHEN DRIVING THROUGH YOUR HOMETOWN. POINT OUT HOT SPOTS—LIKE WHERE YOU BOUGHT GROCERIES.

SIGNED WITNESS

COMPLETED SUCCESSFULLY ☐

YET TO DO ☐

CERTIFIED EXPERT ☐

NOW GIVE IT A REVIEW

☐ HIGHLY RECOMMENDED

☐ IT WAS ENJOYABLE

☐ NOT WORTH THE TIME

HOW MANY STARS?

☆ ☆ ☆ ☆ ☆

___ OUT OF FIVE

SAY 'DO YOU WANT TO PICK UP THIS ONE?' TO YOUR FOUR-YEAR-OLD WHEN THE WAITER BRINGS THE BILL.

SIGNED WITNESS

COMPLETED SUCCESSFULLY ☐

YET TO DO ☐

CERTIFIED EXPERT ☐

NOW GIVE IT A REVIEW

☐ HIGHLY RECOMMENDED

☐ IT WAS ENJOYABLE

☐ NOT WORTH THE TIME

HOW MANY STARS?

☆ ☆ ☆ ☆ ☆

___ OUT OF FIVE

LOOK FORWARD TO THE WEEKEND TO GET AWAY FROM WORK, THEN LOOK FORWARD TO MONDAY TO GET AWAY FROM KIDS.

☐ COMPLETED SUCCESSFULLY

☐ YET TO DO

☐ CERTIFIED EXPERT

SIGNED WITNESS

WITNESS REENACTMENT (SKETCH)

NOW GIVE IT A REVIEW

HOW MANY STARS?

☆ ☆ ☆ ☆ ☆

— OUT OF FIVE

HIGHLY RECOMMENDED ☐

IT WAS ENJOYABLE ☐

NOT WORTH THE TIME ☐

MANDATORY DAD CLICHÉ • NO. 97

COMPLETELY ROAST YOUR WIFE—BUT TOTALLY
MAKE IT ALL BETTER BY QUICKLY SAYING 'YOU
KNOW I LOVE YOUR MOTHER VERY MUCH.'

	COMPLETED SUCCESSFULLY ☐
	YET TO DO ☐
SIGNED WITNESS	CERTIFIED EXPERT ☐

MANDATORY DAD CLICHÉ • NO. 98

GROAN UNNECESSARILY LOUDLY WHEN
DOING STRENUOUS ACTIVITIES LIKE SITTING
IN A CHAIR.

	COMPLETED SUCCESSFULLY ☐
	YET TO DO ☐
SIGNED WITNESS	CERTIFIED EXPERT ☐

MANDATORY DAD CLICHÉ • NO. 99

WALK INTO THE HALLWAY TO ASK
YOUR FAMILY A QUESTION—DESPITE NOT
WEARING PANTS.

	COMPLETED SUCCESSFULLY ☐
	YET TO DO ☐
SIGNED WITNESS	CERTIFIED EXPERT ☐

AFTER A PARTICULARLY INTENSE VISIT TO THE BATHROOM, LIGHT A MATCH. VOILÁ, NO ONE WILL SUSPECT A THING.

☐ COMPLETED SUCCESSFULLY

☐ YET TO DO

☐ CERTIFIED EXPERT

SIGNED WITNESS

NOW GIVE IT A REVIEW

HOW MANY STARS?

☆ ☆ ☆ ☆ ☆

___ OUT OF FIVE

HIGHLY RECOMMENDED ☐

IT WAS ENJOYABLE ☐

NOT WORTH THE TIME ☐

JOIN IN ON SCOLDING YOUR KID FOR SNEAKING THE COOKIES THAT YOU HAVE ALSO ILLEGALLY SNEAKED.

☐ COMPLETED SUCCESSFULLY

☐ YET TO DO

☐ CERTIFIED EXPERT

SIGNED WITNESS

NOW GIVE IT A REVIEW

HOW MANY STARS?

☆ ☆ ☆ ☆ ☆

___ OUT OF FIVE

HIGHLY RECOMMENDED ☐

IT WAS ENJOYABLE ☐

NOT WORTH THE TIME ☐

WHEN SOMEONE ASKS WHAT YOU WANT FOR YOUR BIRTHDAY, GIVE THEM SUPER HELPFUL SUGGESTIONS—LIKE 50 BAGS OF MULCH.

COMPLETED SUCCESSFULLY ☐

YET TO DO ☐

CERTIFIED EXPERT ☐

SIGNED WITNESS

WITNESS REENACTMENT (SKETCH)

NOW GIVE IT A REVIEW

☐ HIGHLY RECOMMENDED

☐ IT WAS ENJOYABLE

☐ NOT WORTH THE TIME

HOW MANY STARS?

☆ ☆ ☆ ☆ ☆

___ OUT OF FIVE

LAUGH WHILE REPRIMANDING YOUR CHILD, FURTHER ENCOURAGING THEM TO DO WHATEVER DUMB THING THEY DID EVEN MORE.

☐ COMPLETED SUCCESSFULLY

☐ YET TO DO

☐ CERTIFIED EXPERT

SIGNED WITNESS

WITNESS REENACTMENT (SKETCH)

NOW GIVE IT A REVIEW

HOW MANY STARS?

☆☆☆☆☆

—— OUT OF FIVE

HIGHLY RECOMMENDED ☐

IT WAS ENJOYABLE ☐

NOT WORTH THE TIME ☐

ENFORCE STRICT CURFEWS AND SCREENINGS OF ALL FRIENDS FOR THE FIRST CHILD. LET THE SECOND KID RUN FERAL.

SIGNED WITNESS

COMPLETED SUCCESSFULLY ☐

YET TO DO ☐

CERTIFIED EXPERT ☐

NOW GIVE IT A REVIEW

☐ HIGHLY RECOMMENDED

☐ IT WAS ENJOYABLE

☐ NOT WORTH THE TIME

HOW MANY STARS?

☆ ☆ ☆ ☆ ☆

___ OUT OF FIVE

CARRY AROUND A WALLET THAT IS THICKER THAN MOST BIBLES—DESPITE THE FACT THAT YOU CARRY NO CASH & USE ONE CREDIT CARD.

SIGNED WITNESS

COMPLETED SUCCESSFULLY ☐

YET TO DO ☐

CERTIFIED EXPERT ☐

NOW GIVE IT A REVIEW

☐ HIGHLY RECOMMENDED

☐ IT WAS ENJOYABLE

☐ NOT WORTH THE TIME

HOW MANY STARS?

☆ ☆ ☆ ☆ ☆

___ OUT OF FIVE

MANDATORY DAD CLICHÉ • NO. 106

IMMEDIATELY FALL ASLEEP AS SOON AS YOU SIT DOWN ON A COUCH. OR A RECLINER. OR A LAWN CHAIR. OR A STOOL. OR THE STAIRS.

- [ ] COMPLETED SUCCESSFULLY
- [ ] YET TO DO
- [ ] CERTIFIED EXPERT

SIGNED WITNESS

MANDATORY DAD CLICHÉ • NO. 107

RECEIVE PRAISE AND APPLAUSE FOR SINGLE-HANDEDLY TAKING CARE OF YOUR OWN CHILD FOR A WHOLE DAY.

- [ ] COMPLETED SUCCESSFULLY
- [ ] YET TO DO
- [ ] CERTIFIED EXPERT

SIGNED WITNESS

MANDATORY DAD CLICHÉ • NO. 108

EXPRESS YOUR DISDAIN FOR TIKTOK WHILE YOUR KIDS PICTURE YOU PLAYING HOOP & STICK DURING THE GREAT DEPRESSION.

- [ ] COMPLETED SUCCESSFULLY
- [ ] YET TO DO
- [ ] CERTIFIED EXPERT

SIGNED WITNESS

MYSTERIOUSLY START GETTING CHARLEY HORSES—NO MATTER THE FACT THAT YOU LAST HAD A GLASS OF WATER IN 1997.

SIGNED WITNESS

COMPLETED SUCCESSFULLY ☐

YET TO DO ☐

CERTIFIED EXPERT ☐

WITNESS REENACTMENT (SKETCH)

NOW GIVE IT A REVIEW

☐ HIGHLY RECOMMENDED

☐ IT WAS ENJOYABLE

☐ NOT WORTH THE TIME

HOW MANY STARS?

☆☆☆☆☆

___ OUT OF FIVE

START A LIGHTHEARTED SNOWBALL FIGHT WITH YOUR KIDS—THAT WILL INEVITABLY END WITH THEM CRYING.

☐ COMPLETED SUCCESSFULLY

☐ YET TO DO

☐ CERTIFIED EXPERT

SIGNED WITNESS

WITNESS REENACTMENT (SKETCH)

NOW GIVE IT A REVIEW

HOW MANY STARS?

☆ ☆ ☆ ☆ ☆

— OUT OF FIVE

HIGHLY RECOMMENDED ☐

IT WAS ENJOYABLE ☐

NOT WORTH THE TIME ☐

FORGET TO PICK UP YOUR KID AT SCHOOL, BUT TOTALLY REMEMBER TO PICK UP SOME MORE CHIPS AT THE STORE.

SIGNED WITNESS

COMPLETED SUCCESSFULLY ☐

YET TO DO ☐

CERTIFIED EXPERT ☐

NOW GIVE IT A REVIEW

☐ HIGHLY RECOMMENDED

☐ IT WAS ENJOYABLE

☐ NOT WORTH THE TIME

HOW MANY STARS?

☆ ☆ ☆ ☆ ☆

___ OUT OF FIVE

SAY 'THEY'RE REALLY BITING TODAY, HUH?' WHEN TALKING ABOUT FISH AND/OR MOSQUITOES.

SIGNED WITNESS

COMPLETED SUCCESSFULLY ☐

YET TO DO ☐

CERTIFIED EXPERT ☐

NOW GIVE IT A REVIEW

☐ HIGHLY RECOMMENDED

☐ IT WAS ENJOYABLE

☐ NOT WORTH THE TIME

HOW MANY STARS?

☆ ☆ ☆ ☆ ☆

___ OUT OF FIVE

HAVE A SUPERNATURAL ABILITY TO LOCATE THE NEAREST BENCH WHENEVER FORCED TO GO CLOTHES SHOPPING W/ THE FAMILY.

☐ COMPLETED SUCCESSFULLY

☐ YET TO DO

☐ CERTIFIED EXPERT

SIGNED WITNESS

WITNESS REENACTMENT (SKETCH)

NOW GIVE IT A REVIEW

HOW MANY STARS?

☆☆☆☆☆

___ OUT OF FIVE

HIGHLY RECOMMENDED ☐

IT WAS ENJOYABLE ☐

NOT WORTH THE TIME ☐

MANDATORY DAD CLICHÉ • NO. 114

SIMULTANEOUSLY BE A GREAT ROLE MODEL AND A HORRIBLE INFLUENCE ON YOUR CHILDREN.

SIGNED WITNESS

COMPLETED SUCCESSFULLY ☐

YET TO DO ☐

CERTIFIED EXPERT ☐

MANDATORY DAD CLICHÉ • NO. 115

VEHEMENTLY DENY FALLING ASLEEP IN THE MOVIE THEATER—IT'S JUST A COINCIDENCE THAT YOUR FAVORITE PART HAPPENED 5 MINUTES IN.

SIGNED WITNESS

COMPLETED SUCCESSFULLY ☐

YET TO DO ☐

CERTIFIED EXPERT ☐

MANDATORY DAD CLICHÉ • NO. 116

WHEN YOUR FAVORITE SONG COMES ON, LOUDLY SING ALONG TO THE THREE WORDS YOU REMEMBER—THEN HUM EVERYTHING ELSE.

SIGNED WITNESS

COMPLETED SUCCESSFULLY ☐

YET TO DO ☐

CERTIFIED EXPERT ☐

MANDATORY DAD CLICHÉ • NO. 117

SAY 'WELL THAT WAS FAST' EVERY TIME
SOMEONE WALKS OUT A DOOR BUT HAS TO COME
BACK BECAUSE THEY FORGOT SOMETHING.

☐ COMPLETED SUCCESSFULLY

☐ YET TO DO

☐ CERTIFIED EXPERT

SIGNED WITNESS

NOW GIVE IT A REVIEW

HOW MANY STARS?
☆ ☆ ☆ ☆ ☆
— OUT OF FIVE

HIGHLY RECOMMENDED ☐

IT WAS ENJOYABLE ☐

NOT WORTH THE TIME ☐

MANDATORY DAD CLICHÉ • NO. 118

PARK IN THE BACK OF EVERY LOT, FAR AWAY
FROM OTHER CARS. SOMEONE MIGHT DING YOUR
2004 TAURUS—IT'S NOT WORTH THE RISK.

☐ COMPLETED SUCCESSFULLY

☐ YET TO DO

☐ CERTIFIED EXPERT

SIGNED WITNESS

NOW GIVE IT A REVIEW

HOW MANY STARS?
☆ ☆ ☆ ☆ ☆
— OUT OF FIVE

HIGHLY RECOMMENDED ☐

IT WAS ENJOYABLE ☐

NOT WORTH THE TIME ☐

RESPOND TO EVERY SINGLE TEXT MESSAGE WITH THE WORD 'OK.'

SIGNED WITNESS

COMPLETED SUCCESSFULLY ☐

YET TO DO ☐

CERTIFIED EXPERT ☐

NOW GIVE IT A REVIEW

☐ HIGHLY RECOMMENDED

☐ IT WAS ENJOYABLE

☐ NOT WORTH THE TIME

HOW MANY STARS?

☆☆☆☆☆

____ OUT OF FIVE

GO ON A FAMILY VACATION, BUT EXCLUSIVELY TALK ABOUT HOW THE PRICE OF GAS HERE COMPARES TO BACK HOME.

SIGNED WITNESS

COMPLETED SUCCESSFULLY ☐

YET TO DO ☐

CERTIFIED EXPERT ☐

NOW GIVE IT A REVIEW

☐ HIGHLY RECOMMENDED

☐ IT WAS ENJOYABLE

☐ NOT WORTH THE TIME

HOW MANY STARS?

☆☆☆☆☆

____ OUT OF FIVE

WHEN ANYTHING BREAKS, FOR ANY REASON WHATSOEVER, SHAKE YOUR HEAD & SAY 'THEY JUST DON'T MAKE THEM LIKE THEY USED TO.'

☐ COMPLETED SUCCESSFULLY

☐ YET TO DO

☐ CERTIFIED EXPERT

SIGNED WITNESS

WITNESS REENACTMENT (SKETCH)

NOW GIVE IT A REVIEW

HOW MANY STARS?

☆☆☆☆☆

—— OUT OF FIVE

HIGHLY RECOMMENDED ☐

IT WAS ENJOYABLE ☐

NOT WORTH THE TIME ☐

TAKING THE KIDS TO THE BEACH FOR THE DAY? WELL DON'T WORRY ABOUT PACKING SUNSCREEN, YOU PROBABLY WON'T NEED IT.

SIGNED WITNESS

COMPLETED SUCCESSFULLY ☐

YET TO DO ☐

CERTIFIED EXPERT ☐

WITNESS REENACTMENT (SKETCH)

NOW GIVE IT A REVIEW

☐ HIGHLY RECOMMENDED

☐ IT WAS ENJOYABLE

☐ NOT WORTH THE TIME

HOW MANY STARS?

☆☆☆☆☆

___ OUT OF FIVE

MANDATORY DAD CLICHÉ • NO. 123

GET SENT TO THE STORE TO PICK UP MILK. RETURN WITH FOUR VARIETIES OF POP-TARTS, A BLOCK OF CHEDDAR CHEESE, & NO MILK.

- [ ] COMPLETED SUCCESSFULLY
- [ ] YET TO DO
- [ ] CERTIFIED EXPERT

SIGNED WITNESS

MANDATORY DAD CLICHÉ • NO. 124

REWARD A SERVER FOR THEIR EXEMPLARY SERVICE WITH A SIXTEEN PERCENT TIP—INSTEAD OF THE USUAL FIFTEEN.

- [ ] COMPLETED SUCCESSFULLY
- [ ] YET TO DO
- [ ] CERTIFIED EXPERT

SIGNED WITNESS

MANDATORY DAD CLICHÉ • NO. 125

ASK FOR 'JUST ONE BITE' OF YOUR KIDS FOOD—WHICH ENDS UP BEING APPROXIMATELY HALF OF THE HOT DOG.

- [ ] COMPLETED SUCCESSFULLY
- [ ] YET TO DO
- [ ] CERTIFIED EXPERT

SIGNED WITNESS

TELL YOUR KIDS THAT THEY NEED TO START
LEARNING HOW TO DO THINGS FOR THEMSELVES.
GET MAD AT THEM FOR DOING IT WRONG.

COMPLETED SUCCESSFULLY ☐

YET TO DO ☐

CERTIFIED EXPERT ☐

SIGNED WITNESS

WITNESS REENACTMENT (SKETCH)

NOW GIVE IT A REVIEW

☐ HIGHLY RECOMMENDED

☐ IT WAS ENJOYABLE

☐ NOT WORTH THE TIME

HOW MANY STARS?

☆☆☆☆☆

____ OUT OF FIVE

IF YOUR CHILD IS ACTING UP, THREATEN TO COUNT TO FIVE—BUT HAVE NO REAL PLAN FOR WHAT TO DO IF YOU ACTUALLY GET THERE.

☐ COMPLETED SUCCESSFULLY

☐ YET TO DO

☐ CERTIFIED EXPERT

SIGNED WITNESS

WITNESS REENACTMENT (SKETCH)

NOW GIVE IT A REVIEW

HOW MANY STARS?

☆☆☆☆☆

— OUT OF FIVE

HIGHLY RECOMMENDED ☐

IT WAS ENJOYABLE ☐

NOT WORTH THE TIME ☐

MANDATORY DAD CLICHÉ • NO. 128

RELENTLESSLY TEASE & MAKE FUN OF YOUR KIDS FOR YEARS—YET IMMEDIATELY GET MAD IF THEY DARE TEASE YOU BACK.

	COMPLETED SUCCESSFULLY ☐
	YET TO DO ☐
SIGNED WITNESS	CERTIFIED EXPERT ☐

NOW GIVE IT A REVIEW

☐ HIGHLY RECOMMENDED

☐ IT WAS ENJOYABLE

☐ NOT WORTH THE TIME

HOW MANY STARS?

☆ ☆ ☆ ☆ ☆

___ OUT OF FIVE

MANDATORY DAD CLICHÉ • NO. 129

SAY 'YOU'LL UNDERSTAND WHEN YOU'RE OLDER' WHEN ASKED ABOUT SOMETHING THAT YOU DON'T REALLY UNDERSTAND EITHER.

	COMPLETED SUCCESSFULLY ☐
	YET TO DO ☐
SIGNED WITNESS	CERTIFIED EXPERT ☐

NOW GIVE IT A REVIEW

☐ HIGHLY RECOMMENDED

☐ IT WAS ENJOYABLE

☐ NOT WORTH THE TIME

HOW MANY STARS?

☆ ☆ ☆ ☆ ☆

___ OUT OF FIVE

INSPIRE YOUR KIDS TO PURSUE HIGHER EDUCATION BY ENTHRALLING THEM WITH YOUR MUNDANE STORIES ABOUT COLLEGE.

- [ ] COMPLETED SUCCESSFULLY
- [ ] YET TO DO
- [ ] CERTIFIED EXPERT

SIGNED WITNESS

NOW GIVE IT A REVIEW

HOW MANY STARS?

☆ ☆ ☆ ☆ ☆

___ OUT OF FIVE

HIGHLY RECOMMENDED [ ]

IT WAS ENJOYABLE [ ]

NOT WORTH THE TIME [ ]

NO MATTER HOW SEVERE YOUR CHILD'S INJURY IS, SLAP A BAND-AID ON IT AND TELL THEM THAT THEY'LL BE FINE.

- [ ] COMPLETED SUCCESSFULLY
- [ ] YET TO DO
- [ ] CERTIFIED EXPERT

SIGNED WITNESS

NOW GIVE IT A REVIEW

HOW MANY STARS?

☆ ☆ ☆ ☆ ☆

___ OUT OF FIVE

HIGHLY RECOMMENDED [ ]

IT WAS ENJOYABLE [ ]

NOT WORTH THE TIME [ ]

MESS UP PUTTING ON THE BABY'S DIAPER—BUT IT'S NOTHING THAT A LITTLE PACKING TAPE WON'T FIX.

SIGNED WITNESS

COMPLETED SUCCESSFULLY ☐

YET TO DO ☐

CERTIFIED EXPERT ☐

WITNESS REENACTMENT (SKETCH)

NOW GIVE IT A REVIEW

☐ HIGHLY RECOMMENDED

☐ IT WAS ENJOYABLE

☐ NOT WORTH THE TIME

HOW MANY STARS?

☆☆☆☆☆

___ OUT OF FIVE

START SHOVELING THE DRIVEWAY AS SOON AS THE FIRST SNOWFLAKE LANDS ON THE GROUND.

☐ COMPLETED SUCCESSFULLY

☐ YET TO DO

☐ CERTIFIED EXPERT

SIGNED WITNESS

WITNESS REENACTMENT (SKETCH)

NOW GIVE IT A REVIEW

HOW MANY STARS?

☆☆☆☆☆

— OUT OF FIVE

HIGHLY RECOMMENDED ☐

IT WAS ENJOYABLE ☐

NOT WORTH THE TIME ☐

MANDATORY DAD CLICHÉ • NO. 134

DRINK THE LAST OF THE MILK AND PUT
THE EMPTY CARTON BACK IN THE FRIDGE.
BLAME YOUR KID.

SIGNED WITNESS

COMPLETED SUCCESSFULLY ☐

YET TO DO ☐

CERTIFIED EXPERT ☐

MANDATORY DAD CLICHÉ • NO. 135

RELEASE A SILENT & UNEXPECTEDLY POTENT
FART IN THE LIVING ROOM AFTER DINNER.
BLAME THE DOG.

SIGNED WITNESS

COMPLETED SUCCESSFULLY ☐

YET TO DO ☐

CERTIFIED EXPERT ☐

MANDATORY DAD CLICHÉ • NO. 136

MISTAKENLY AGREE TO A SECOND CHILD.
BLAME YOURSELF.

SIGNED WITNESS

COMPLETED SUCCESSFULLY ☐

YET TO DO ☐

CERTIFIED EXPERT ☐

PROUDLY WEAR A FANNY PACK—RIGHT ABOVE YOUR CROTCH. KEEP SOME SALTINES IN THERE TOO, FOR UNKNOWN REASONS.

- [ ] COMPLETED SUCCESSFULLY
- [ ] YET TO DO
- [ ] CERTIFIED EXPERT

SIGNED WITNESS

NOW GIVE IT A REVIEW

HOW MANY STARS?
☆ ☆ ☆ ☆ ☆
— OUT OF FIVE

- HIGHLY RECOMMENDED [ ]
- IT WAS ENJOYABLE [ ]
- NOT WORTH THE TIME [ ]

TEACH YOUR KIDS NOT TO TALK TO STRANGERS—WHILE MAKING SMALL TALK WITH EVERY STRANGER WITHIN A 50 FOOT RADIUS.

- [ ] COMPLETED SUCCESSFULLY
- [ ] YET TO DO
- [ ] CERTIFIED EXPERT

SIGNED WITNESS

NOW GIVE IT A REVIEW

HOW MANY STARS?
☆ ☆ ☆ ☆ ☆
— OUT OF FIVE

- HIGHLY RECOMMENDED [ ]
- IT WAS ENJOYABLE [ ]
- NOT WORTH THE TIME [ ]

DRAG YOUR KID ON A CAMPING TRIP THEY HAVE ZERO INTEREST IN. BE SURE TO DRONE ON AND ON ABOUT THE SUNSET OR WHATEVER.

SIGNED WITNESS

COMPLETED SUCCESSFULLY ☐

YET TO DO ☐

CERTIFIED EXPERT ☐

WITNESS REENACTMENT (SKETCH)

NOW GIVE IT A REVIEW

☐ HIGHLY RECOMMENDED

☐ IT WAS ENJOYABLE

☐ NOT WORTH THE TIME

HOW MANY STARS?

☆ ☆ ☆ ☆ ☆

___ OUT OF FIVE

SPEND THOUSANDS OF DOLLARS ON A BIG FAMILY VACATION, BUT MAKE EVERYONE SHARE A SINGLE CUP OF ICE CREAM.

☐ COMPLETED SUCCESSFULLY

☐ YET TO DO

☐ CERTIFIED EXPERT

SIGNED WITNESS

WITNESS REENACTMENT (SKETCH)

NOW GIVE IT A REVIEW

HOW MANY STARS?

☆ ☆ ☆ ☆ ☆

— OUT OF FIVE

HIGHLY RECOMMENDED ☐

IT WAS ENJOYABLE ☐

NOT WORTH THE TIME ☐

TIME TO CARVE PUMPKINS? PULL OUT THE LARGE KITCHEN KNIVES, WITHOUT EVEN A HINT OF UNDERSTANDING WHY THAT'S A BAD IDEA.

SIGNED WITNESS

COMPLETED SUCCESSFULLY ☐

YET TO DO ☐

CERTIFIED EXPERT ☐

NOW GIVE IT A REVIEW

☐ HIGHLY RECOMMENDED

☐ IT WAS ENJOYABLE

☐ NOT WORTH THE TIME

HOW MANY STARS?

☆☆☆☆☆

___ OUT OF FIVE

YELL AT YOUR KIDS FOR BEING SLIGHTLY BETTER BEHAVED THAN YOU WERE AT THAT AGE.

SIGNED WITNESS

COMPLETED SUCCESSFULLY ☐

YET TO DO ☐

CERTIFIED EXPERT ☐

NOW GIVE IT A REVIEW

☐ HIGHLY RECOMMENDED

☐ IT WAS ENJOYABLE

☐ NOT WORTH THE TIME

HOW MANY STARS?

☆☆☆☆☆

___ OUT OF FIVE

MANDATORY DAD CLICHÉ • NO. 143

**SAY THINGS LIKE 'TIME IS MONEY'—THEN
SPEND 45 MINUTES IN THE BATHROOM READING
THE ENTIRETY OF A MAGAZINE.**

☐ COMPLETED SUCCESSFULLY

☐ YET TO DO

☐ CERTIFIED EXPERT

SIGNED WITNESS

MANDATORY DAD CLICHÉ • NO. 144

**DROP A HAMBURGER ON THE GROUND WHILE
GRILLING. NOW MAKE SURE NO ONE IS LOOKING,
DUST IT OFF, AND PUT IT BACK ON THE GRILL.**

☐ COMPLETED SUCCESSFULLY

☐ YET TO DO

☐ CERTIFIED EXPERT

SIGNED WITNESS

MANDATORY DAD CLICHÉ • NO. 145

**RUN INTO A MINOR ACQUAINTANCE AT THE
GROCERY STORE—MAKE YOUR KID STAND THERE
SILENTLY FOR AN HOUR WHILE YOU CATCH UP.**

☐ COMPLETED SUCCESSFULLY

☐ YET TO DO

☐ CERTIFIED EXPERT

SIGNED WITNESS

MANDATORY DAD CLICHÉ • NO. 146

PUSH YOUR KID AS HIGH AS POSSIBLE ON THE SWING SET—MUCH TO THEIR TERROR, THEN DELIGHT, THEN TERROR AGAIN.

SIGNED WITNESS

COMPLETED SUCCESSFULLY ☐

YET TO DO ☐

CERTIFIED EXPERT ☐

NOW GIVE IT A REVIEW

☐ HIGHLY RECOMMENDED

☐ IT WAS ENJOYABLE

☐ NOT WORTH THE TIME

HOW MANY STARS?

☆ ☆ ☆ ☆ ☆

___ OUT OF FIVE

MANDATORY DAD CLICHÉ • NO. 147

HAVE A FLIGHT TODAY? WELL, BETTER GET TO THE AIRPORT FOUR HOURS EARLY—JUST IN CASE THERE IS A LINE.

SIGNED WITNESS

COMPLETED SUCCESSFULLY ☐

YET TO DO ☐

CERTIFIED EXPERT ☐

NOW GIVE IT A REVIEW

☐ HIGHLY RECOMMENDED

☐ IT WAS ENJOYABLE

☐ NOT WORTH THE TIME

HOW MANY STARS?

☆ ☆ ☆ ☆ ☆

___ OUT OF FIVE

BUY ALL GIFTS NO MORE THAN 24 HOURS BEFORE THE EVENT, & WRAP THEM NO EARLIER THAN 30 SECONDS PRIOR TO GIVING THEM.

- [ ] COMPLETED SUCCESSFULLY
- [ ] YET TO DO
- [ ] CERTIFIED EXPERT

SIGNED WITNESS

NOW GIVE IT A REVIEW

HOW MANY STARS?
☆ ☆ ☆ ☆ ☆
___ OUT OF FIVE

- HIGHLY RECOMMENDED [ ]
- IT WAS ENJOYABLE [ ]
- NOT WORTH THE TIME [ ]

CALL WHATEVER YOUR KID DOES FOR FUN A WASTE OF TIME. NOW MAKE THEM GO FISHING WITH YOU—CATCH AND RELEASE OF COURSE.

- [ ] COMPLETED SUCCESSFULLY
- [ ] YET TO DO
- [ ] CERTIFIED EXPERT

SIGNED WITNESS

NOW GIVE IT A REVIEW

HOW MANY STARS?
☆ ☆ ☆ ☆ ☆
___ OUT OF FIVE

- HIGHLY RECOMMENDED [ ]
- IT WAS ENJOYABLE [ ]
- NOT WORTH THE TIME [ ]

FORCE THE KIDS TO GO OUTSIDE & ENJOY THE DAY—WHILE SITTING IN THE AIR CONDITIONING BECAUSE IT'S FREAKING HOT OUT THERE.

SIGNED WITNESS

COMPLETED SUCCESSFULLY ☐

YET TO DO ☐

CERTIFIED EXPERT ☐

WITNESS REENACTMENT (SKETCH)

NOW GIVE IT A REVIEW

☐ HIGHLY RECOMMENDED

☐ IT WAS ENJOYABLE

☐ NOT WORTH THE TIME

HOW MANY STARS?

☆☆☆☆☆

___ OUT OF FIVE

PATIENTLY TEACH YOUR KIDS TO DRIVE A STICK SHIFT–IN YOUR IMAGINATION–BEFORE ACTUALLY YELLING 'STOP RIDING THE CLUTCH!'

- [ ] COMPLETED SUCCESSFULLY
- [ ] YET TO DO
- [ ] CERTIFIED EXPERT

SIGNED WITNESS

WITNESS REENACTMENT (SKETCH)

NOW GIVE IT A REVIEW

HOW MANY STARS?

☆ ☆ ☆ ☆ ☆

___ OUT OF FIVE

HIGHLY RECOMMENDED [ ]

IT WAS ENJOYABLE [ ]

NOT WORTH THE TIME [ ]

MANDATORY DAD CLICHÉ · NO. 152

REPEATEDLY EXPLAIN HOW 'DO WHAT YOU LOVE AND YOU'LL NEVER WORK A DAY IN YOUR LIFE' IS COMPLETE BULLSHIT.

SIGNED WITNESS

COMPLETED SUCCESSFULLY ☐

YET TO DO ☐

CERTIFIED EXPERT ☐

NOW GIVE IT A REVIEW

☐ HIGHLY RECOMMENDED

☐ IT WAS ENJOYABLE

☐ NOT WORTH THE TIME

HOW MANY STARS?

☆ ☆ ☆ ☆ ☆

___ OUT OF FIVE

MANDATORY DAD CLICHÉ · NO. 153

PLAY CHESS WITH YOUR KID & LET THEM WIN. YOU KNOW, SO THEY CAN FEEL BETTER ABOUT THEMSELVES...NOT BECAUSE YOU SUCK AT IT.

SIGNED WITNESS

COMPLETED SUCCESSFULLY ☐

YET TO DO ☐

CERTIFIED EXPERT ☐

NOW GIVE IT A REVIEW

☐ HIGHLY RECOMMENDED

☐ IT WAS ENJOYABLE

☐ NOT WORTH THE TIME

HOW MANY STARS?

☆ ☆ ☆ ☆ ☆

___ OUT OF FIVE

MOW THE LAWN EVERY SINGLE WEEKEND, NO MATTER IF THE GRASS HAS ACTUALLY GROWN OR NOT.

☐ COMPLETED SUCCESSFULLY

☐ YET TO DO

☐ CERTIFIED EXPERT

SIGNED WITNESS

NOW GIVE IT A REVIEW

HOW MANY STARS?

☆☆☆☆☆

___ OUT OF FIVE

HIGHLY RECOMMENDED ☐

IT WAS ENJOYABLE ☐

NOT WORTH THE TIME ☐

SAY STUFF LIKE 'THAT'S GOOD ENOUGH FOR GOVERNMENT WORK' W/ NO ACTUAL IDEA WHAT IT MEANS—OTHER THAN YOU DID A TERRIBLE JOB.

☐ COMPLETED SUCCESSFULLY

☐ YET TO DO

☐ CERTIFIED EXPERT

SIGNED WITNESS

NOW GIVE IT A REVIEW

HOW MANY STARS?

☆☆☆☆☆

___ OUT OF FIVE

HIGHLY RECOMMENDED ☐

IT WAS ENJOYABLE ☐

NOT WORTH THE TIME ☐

MANDATORY DAD CLICHÉ • NO. 156

WHENEVER YOU SEE ANYBODY OUTSIDE WASHING THEIR CAR, GO OUT OF YOUR WAY TO ASK THEM IF THEY CAN DO YOURS NEXT.

SIGNED WITNESS

COMPLETED SUCCESSFULLY ☐

YET TO DO ☐

CERTIFIED EXPERT ☐

MANDATORY DAD CLICHÉ • NO. 157

PUT EVERYTHING TOGETHER WITHOUT READING THE INSTRUCTIONS—JUST THROW AWAY ALL OF THOSE 'EXTRA' PIECES.

SIGNED WITNESS

COMPLETED SUCCESSFULLY ☐

YET TO DO ☐

CERTIFIED EXPERT ☐

MANDATORY DAD CLICHÉ • NO. 158

CHOOSE UNIQUE, AND OBNOXIOUSLY LOUD, RINGTONES FOR EVERY CONTACT IN YOUR PHONE.

SIGNED WITNESS

COMPLETED SUCCESSFULLY ☐

YET TO DO ☐

CERTIFIED EXPERT ☐

CHANGE OUT OF YOUR STAINED SHIRT TO GO OUT TO DINNER, AND IMMEDIATELY SPILL FOOD ON YOUR CLEAN SHIRT.

☐ COMPLETED SUCCESSFULLY

☐ YET TO DO

☐ CERTIFIED EXPERT

SIGNED WITNESS

WITNESS REENACTMENT (SKETCH)

NOW GIVE IT A REVIEW

HOW MANY STARS?

☆ ☆ ☆ ☆ ☆

—— OUT OF FIVE

HIGHLY RECOMMENDED ☐

IT WAS ENJOYABLE ☐

NOT WORTH THE TIME ☐

ANSWER EVERY CALL FROM AN UNKNOWN NUMBER—AND ALWAYS BE SURPRISED THAT IT'S A TELEMARKETER.

SIGNED WITNESS

COMPLETED SUCCESSFULLY ☐

YET TO DO ☐

CERTIFIED EXPERT ☐

WITNESS REENACTMENT (SKETCH)

NOW GIVE IT A REVIEW

☐ HIGHLY RECOMMENDED

☐ IT WAS ENJOYABLE

☐ NOT WORTH THE TIME

HOW MANY STARS?

☆☆☆☆☆

___ OUT OF FIVE

ON PHONE CALLS, ASK ABOUT HOW YOUR KID'S CAR IS DOING MORE THAN YOU ASK ABOUT HOW YOUR ACTUAL KID IS DOING.

- ☐ COMPLETED SUCCESSFULLY
- ☐ YET TO DO
- ☐ CERTIFIED EXPERT

SIGNED WITNESS

NOW GIVE IT A REVIEW

HOW MANY STARS?

☆ ☆ ☆ ☆ ☆

—— OUT OF FIVE

HIGHLY RECOMMENDED ☐

IT WAS ENJOYABLE ☐

NOT WORTH THE TIME ☐

SAY THINGS LIKE 'IT'S NOT HEAVY, IT'S JUST AWKWARD' WHEN YOU'RE CARRYING SOMETHING THAT IS OBVIOUSLY TOO HEAVY.

- ☐ COMPLETED SUCCESSFULLY
- ☐ YET TO DO
- ☐ CERTIFIED EXPERT

SIGNED WITNESS

NOW GIVE IT A REVIEW

HOW MANY STARS?

☆ ☆ ☆ ☆ ☆

—— OUT OF FIVE

HIGHLY RECOMMENDED ☐

IT WAS ENJOYABLE ☐

NOT WORTH THE TIME ☐

AIMLESSLY WANDER AROUND A STORE FOR 30 MINUTES LOOKING FOR AN ITEM RATHER THAN ASK AN EMPLOYEE.

COMPLETED SUCCESSFULLY ☐

YET TO DO ☐

CERTIFIED EXPERT ☐

SIGNED WITNESS

WITNESS REENACTMENT (SKETCH)

NOW GIVE IT A REVIEW

☐ HIGHLY RECOMMENDED

☐ IT WAS ENJOYABLE

☐ NOT WORTH THE TIME

HOW MANY STARS?

☆ ☆ ☆ ☆ ☆

___ OUT OF FIVE

MANDATORY DAD CLICHÉ • NO. 164

KEEP IN TOUCH WITH EXACTLY ONE FRIEND FROM COLLEGE, WHOM YOU'VE SEEN MAYBE TWICE IN THE LAST TWO DECADES.

- [ ] COMPLETED SUCCESSFULLY
- [ ] YET TO DO
- [ ] CERTIFIED EXPERT

SIGNED WITNESS

MANDATORY DAD CLICHÉ • NO. 165

WHENEVER YOUR KID DOES SOMETHING BAD, DECLARE THAT THEY MUST HAVE 'LEARNED THAT FROM THEIR MOTHER.'

- [ ] COMPLETED SUCCESSFULLY
- [ ] YET TO DO
- [ ] CERTIFIED EXPERT

SIGNED WITNESS

MANDATORY DAD CLICHÉ • NO. 166

DRESS UP LIKE A PRINCESS TO HAVE A TEA PARTY—MAYBE EVEN INVITE YOUR KIDS.

- [ ] COMPLETED SUCCESSFULLY
- [ ] YET TO DO
- [ ] CERTIFIED EXPERT

SIGNED WITNESS

MANDATORY DAD CLICHÉ · NO. 167

START THOUSANDS OF DIFFERENT PROJECTS AROUND THE HOUSE. NEVER FINISH A SINGLE ONE OF THEM.

SIGNED WITNESS

COMPLETED SUCCESSFULLY ☐

YET TO DO ☐

CERTIFIED EXPERT ☐

NOW GIVE IT A REVIEW

☐ HIGHLY RECOMMENDED

☐ IT WAS ENJOYABLE

☐ NOT WORTH THE TIME

HOW MANY STARS?

☆ ☆ ☆ ☆ ☆

___ OUT OF FIVE

MANDATORY DAD CLICHÉ · NO. 168

HELP YOUR KID A LITTLE BIT WITH THEIR SCIENCE FAIR PROJECT BY COMPLETELY TAKING IT OVER & DOING THE WHOLE THING ALONE.

SIGNED WITNESS

COMPLETED SUCCESSFULLY ☐

YET TO DO ☐

CERTIFIED EXPERT ☐

NOW GIVE IT A REVIEW

☐ HIGHLY RECOMMENDED

☐ IT WAS ENJOYABLE

☐ NOT WORTH THE TIME

HOW MANY STARS?

☆ ☆ ☆ ☆ ☆

___ OUT OF FIVE

KEEP ALL OF YOUR TOOLS NEATLY ORGANIZED IN ONE GIANT PILE ON THE TOP OF YOUR WORKBENCH.

- [ ] COMPLETED SUCCESSFULLY
- [ ] YET TO DO
- [ ] CERTIFIED EXPERT

SIGNED WITNESS

NOW GIVE IT A REVIEW

HOW MANY STARS?

☆ ☆ ☆ ☆ ☆

___ OUT OF FIVE

- HIGHLY RECOMMENDED [ ]
- IT WAS ENJOYABLE [ ]
- NOT WORTH THE TIME [ ]

SAY 'HEY, I WAS WATCHING THAT' WHENEVER SOMEONE TURNS THE TV OFF IN ANOTHER ROOM THAT YOU HAVEN'T BEEN IN FOR AN HOUR.

- [ ] COMPLETED SUCCESSFULLY
- [ ] YET TO DO
- [ ] CERTIFIED EXPERT

SIGNED WITNESS

NOW GIVE IT A REVIEW

HOW MANY STARS?

☆ ☆ ☆ ☆ ☆

___ OUT OF FIVE

- HIGHLY RECOMMENDED [ ]
- IT WAS ENJOYABLE [ ]
- NOT WORTH THE TIME [ ]

MANDATORY DAD CLICHÉ · NO. 171

WEAR A ROBE THAT YOU'RE ALWAYS PRECARIOUSLY CLOSE TO EXPOSING YOURSELF WITH—ESPECIALLY WHEN COMPANY IS AROUND.

SIGNED WITNESS

COMPLETED SUCCESSFULLY ☐

YET TO DO ☐

CERTIFIED EXPERT ☐

WITNESS REENACTMENT (SKETCH)

NOW GIVE IT A REVIEW

☐ HIGHLY RECOMMENDED

☐ IT WAS ENJOYABLE

☐ NOT WORTH THE TIME

HOW MANY STARS?

☆☆☆☆☆

___ OUT OF FIVE

MISPRONOUNCE COMMON WORDS ON PURPOSE, LIKE 'WHO'S HUNGRY? I'LL GRILL UP SOME BURGLERS.' IT'LL NEVER GET OLD...FOR YOU.

- [ ] COMPLETED SUCCESSFULLY
- [ ] YET TO DO
- [ ] CERTIFIED EXPERT

SIGNED WITNESS

WITNESS REENACTMENT (SKETCH)

NOW GIVE IT A REVIEW

HOW MANY STARS?

☆☆☆☆☆

____ OUT OF FIVE

HIGHLY RECOMMENDED [ ]

IT WAS ENJOYABLE [ ]

NOT WORTH THE TIME [ ]

GIVE YOUR KIDS SILLY NICKNAMES THAT THEY'LL THINK ARE HILARIOUS — UNTIL LITTLE 'FISH STICK' TURNS TWENTY-EIGHT ANYWAY.

SIGNED WITNESS

COMPLETED SUCCESSFULLY ☐

YET TO DO ☐

CERTIFIED EXPERT ☐

WITNESS REENACTMENT (SKETCH)

NOW GIVE IT A REVIEW

☐ HIGHLY RECOMMENDED

☐ IT WAS ENJOYABLE

☐ NOT WORTH THE TIME

HOW MANY STARS?

☆ ☆ ☆ ☆ ☆

___ OUT OF FIVE

MANDATORY DAD CLICHÉ · NO. 174

TEACH YOUR KIDS THE QUIET GAME & TELL THEM THAT IF THEY PRACTICE HARD ENOUGH, THEY COULD GO PRO ONE DAY.

☐ COMPLETED SUCCESSFULLY

☐ YET TO DO

☐ CERTIFIED EXPERT

SIGNED WITNESS

MANDATORY DAD CLICHÉ · NO. 175

THREATEN TO SELL YOUR KIDS ON EBAY.

☐ COMPLETED SUCCESSFULLY

☐ YET TO DO

☐ CERTIFIED EXPERT

SIGNED WITNESS

MANDATORY DAD CLICHÉ · NO. 176

HONK THE HORN IF YOU'VE BEEN WAITING LONGER THAN 27 SECONDS FOR YOUR FAMILY TO GET INTO THE CAR.

☐ COMPLETED SUCCESSFULLY

☐ YET TO DO

☐ CERTIFIED EXPERT

SIGNED WITNESS

SAY 'I'M NOT SLEEPING, I'M JUST RESTING MY EYES' AFTER JUST WAKING YOURSELF UP WITH YOUR OWN SNORING.

SIGNED WITNESS

COMPLETED SUCCESSFULLY ☐

YET TO DO ☐

CERTIFIED EXPERT ☐

WITNESS REENACTMENT (SKETCH)

NOW GIVE IT A REVIEW

☐ HIGHLY RECOMMENDED

☐ IT WAS ENJOYABLE

☐ NOT WORTH THE TIME

HOW MANY STARS?

☆☆☆☆☆

___ OUT OF FIVE

HAVE A HUGE COLLECTION OF 'CLASSIC' VHS TAPES THAT YOU REFUSE TO GET RID OF, DESPITE NOT EVEN HAVING A WORKING VCR.

☐ COMPLETED SUCCESSFULLY

☐ YET TO DO

☐ CERTIFIED EXPERT

SIGNED WITNESS

WITNESS REENACTMENT (SKETCH)

NOW GIVE IT A REVIEW

HOW MANY STARS?

☆ ☆ ☆ ☆ ☆

— OUT OF FIVE

HIGHLY RECOMMENDED ☐

IT WAS ENJOYABLE ☐

NOT WORTH THE TIME ☐

EAT A GREAT MEAL? BE SURE TO RUB YOUR BELLY AWKWARDLY FOR AT LEAST TEN MINUTES, JUST TO MAKE SURE EVERYBODY KNOWS.

SIGNED WITNESS

COMPLETED SUCCESSFULLY ☐

YET TO DO ☐

CERTIFIED EXPERT ☐

NOW GIVE IT A REVIEW

☐ HIGHLY RECOMMENDED

☐ IT WAS ENJOYABLE

☐ NOT WORTH THE TIME

HOW MANY STARS?

☆ ☆ ☆ ☆ ☆

___ OUT OF FIVE

DECLARE THAT YOU'RE 'NOT MADE OF MONEY' WHEN YOUR CHILD NEEDS ANYTHING, INCLUDING BASIC FOOD & SHELTER.

SIGNED WITNESS

COMPLETED SUCCESSFULLY ☐

YET TO DO ☐

CERTIFIED EXPERT ☐

NOW GIVE IT A REVIEW

☐ HIGHLY RECOMMENDED

☐ IT WAS ENJOYABLE

☐ NOT WORTH THE TIME

HOW MANY STARS?

☆ ☆ ☆ ☆ ☆

___ OUT OF FIVE

HAVE A CHILD FOR THE SOLE PURPOSE OF EMBARRASSING THEM AS MUCH AS YOUR OWN FATHER EMBARRASSED YOU.

- [ ] COMPLETED SUCCESSFULLY
- [ ] YET TO DO
- [ ] CERTIFIED EXPERT

SIGNED WITNESS

NOW GIVE IT A REVIEW

HOW MANY STARS?

☆ ☆ ☆ ☆ ☆

___ OUT OF FIVE

HIGHLY RECOMMENDED [ ]

IT WAS ENJOYABLE [ ]

NOT WORTH THE TIME [ ]

CAREFULLY TEACH YOUR KID TO RIDE A BIKE WITHOUT TRAINING WHEELS BY JUST LETTING GO AND SEEING WHAT HAPPENS.

- [ ] COMPLETED SUCCESSFULLY
- [ ] YET TO DO
- [ ] CERTIFIED EXPERT

SIGNED WITNESS

NOW GIVE IT A REVIEW

HOW MANY STARS?

☆ ☆ ☆ ☆ ☆

___ OUT OF FIVE

HIGHLY RECOMMENDED [ ]

IT WAS ENJOYABLE [ ]

NOT WORTH THE TIME [ ]

SAY 'YOU'RE GOING TO LOVE THIS ONE' AS YOU SHOW YOUR 5-YEAR-OLD THE MOVIE 'GREMLINS' AND PROCEED TO SCAR THEM FOR LIFE.

COMPLETED SUCCESSFULLY ☐

YET TO DO ☐

CERTIFIED EXPERT ☐

SIGNED WITNESS

WITNESS REENACTMENT (SKETCH)

NOW GIVE IT A REVIEW

☐ HIGHLY RECOMMENDED

☐ IT WAS ENJOYABLE

☐ NOT WORTH THE TIME

HOW MANY STARS?

☆ ☆ ☆ ☆ ☆

___ OUT OF FIVE

OVERHEAR YOUR KID SAYING THEY THINK SOMEONE IS KIND OF CUTE—INSTANTLY SHOUT 'OH MY GOSH, DO YOU LIKE THEM!?!'

☐ COMPLETED SUCCESSFULLY

☐ YET TO DO

☐ CERTIFIED EXPERT

SIGNED WITNESS

WITNESS REENACTMENT (SKETCH)

NOW GIVE IT A REVIEW

HOW MANY STARS?

☆☆☆☆☆

—— OUT OF FIVE

HIGHLY RECOMMENDED ☐

IT WAS ENJOYABLE ☐

NOT WORTH THE TIME ☐

MANDATORY DAD CLICHÉ • NO. 185

TEAR UP WATCHING A SAPPY MOVIE—BUT IF ANYONE NOTICES, BLAME THE ONIONS THAT YOU APPARENTLY CUT WITHOUT ANYONE SEEING.

	COMPLETED SUCCESSFULLY ☐
	YET TO DO ☐
SIGNED WITNESS	CERTIFIED EXPERT ☐

MANDATORY DAD CLICHÉ • NO. 186

REFER TO ANYONE THAT'S MORE THAN A MONTH YOUNGER THAN YOU AS 'CHAMP.'

	COMPLETED SUCCESSFULLY ☐
	YET TO DO ☐
SIGNED WITNESS	CERTIFIED EXPERT ☐

MANDATORY DAD CLICHÉ • NO. 187

TURN OFF EVERY LIGHT IN THE HOUSE RELIGIOUSLY—EVEN THE ONES THAT PEOPLE ARE STILL USING.

	COMPLETED SUCCESSFULLY ☐
	YET TO DO ☐
SIGNED WITNESS	CERTIFIED EXPERT ☐

MANDATORY DAD CLICHÉ • NO. 188

HAVE CAT-LIKE REFLEXES WHEN YOUR KID FALLS OFF OF SOMETHING—YET STILL MANAGE TO SPRAIN YOUR ANKLE WHILE JUST WALKING.

☐ COMPLETED SUCCESSFULLY

☐ YET TO DO

☐ CERTIFIED EXPERT

SIGNED WITNESS

NOW GIVE IT A REVIEW

HOW MANY STARS?

☆☆☆☆☆

___ OUT OF FIVE

HIGHLY RECOMMENDED ☐

IT WAS ENJOYABLE ☐

NOT WORTH THE TIME ☐

MANDATORY DAD CLICHÉ • NO. 189

SAY 'I'M NOT MAD, JUST DISAPPOINTED' WHEN YOU ARE, IN FACT, FURIOUS—BUT TOO TIRED TO CARE ABOUT LITERALLY ANYTHING ANYMORE.

☐ COMPLETED SUCCESSFULLY

☐ YET TO DO

☐ CERTIFIED EXPERT

SIGNED WITNESS

NOW GIVE IT A REVIEW

HOW MANY STARS?

☆☆☆☆☆

___ OUT OF FIVE

HIGHLY RECOMMENDED ☐

IT WAS ENJOYABLE ☐

NOT WORTH THE TIME ☐

FINISH CHANGING THE BABY INTO A FRESH DIAPER & CLOTHES—AND IMMEDIATELY HEAR IT LOSE ANOTHER LOAD. PRETEND YOU DIDN'T.

SIGNED WITNESS

COMPLETED SUCCESSFULLY ☐

YET TO DO ☐

CERTIFIED EXPERT ☐

WITNESS REENACTMENT (SKETCH)

NOW GIVE IT A REVIEW

☐ HIGHLY RECOMMENDED

☐ IT WAS ENJOYABLE

☐ NOT WORTH THE TIME

HOW MANY STARS?

☆ ☆ ☆ ☆ ☆

___ OUT OF FIVE

WHEN YOUR KID SAYS 'CAN I ASK YOU A QUESTION?' RESPOND WITH 'YOU JUST DID!' THEY'LL LOVE IT.

☐ COMPLETED SUCCESSFULLY

☐ YET TO DO

☐ CERTIFIED EXPERT

SIGNED WITNESS

WITNESS REENACTMENT (SKETCH)

NOW GIVE IT A REVIEW

HOW MANY STARS?

☆☆☆☆☆

—— OUT OF FIVE

HIGHLY RECOMMENDED ☐

IT WAS ENJOYABLE ☐

NOT WORTH THE TIME ☐

NEVER FAIL TO IMPRESS YOUR CHILDREN BY SOMEHOW FORGETTING THE NAMES OF FRIENDS THAT THEY'VE HAD FOR TEN YEARS.

SIGNED WITNESS

COMPLETED SUCCESSFULLY ☐

YET TO DO ☐

CERTIFIED EXPERT ☐

NOW GIVE IT A REVIEW

☐ HIGHLY RECOMMENDED

☐ IT WAS ENJOYABLE

☐ NOT WORTH THE TIME

HOW MANY STARS?

☆ ☆ ☆ ☆ ☆

___ OUT OF FIVE

HOVER OVER THE PLUMBER WHILE THEY FIX YOUR SINK, SAYING THINGS LIKE 'YEAH, I JUST DIDN'T HAVE THE RIGHT TOOLS TO DO IT.'

SIGNED WITNESS

COMPLETED SUCCESSFULLY ☐

YET TO DO ☐

CERTIFIED EXPERT ☐

NOW GIVE IT A REVIEW

☐ HIGHLY RECOMMENDED

☐ IT WAS ENJOYABLE

☐ NOT WORTH THE TIME

HOW MANY STARS?

☆ ☆ ☆ ☆ ☆

___ OUT OF FIVE

PLOP A KID IN THE BACK OF A CONVERTIBLE WITHOUT SUNSCREEN & DRIVE FROM OHIO TO FLORIDA IN ONE (EXTREMELY SUNNY) DAY.*

- [ ] COMPLETED SUCCESSFULLY
- [ ] YET TO DO
- [ ] CERTIFIED EXPERT

*OK, SO MAYBE THIS ONE WAS JUST MY DAD.

MISS YOU.

SIGNED WITNESS

NOW GIVE IT A REVIEW

HOW MANY STARS?

☆ ☆ ☆ ☆ ☆

___ OUT OF FIVE

- [ ] HIGHLY RECOMMENDED
- [ ] IT WAS ENJOYABLE
- [ ] NOT WORTH THE TIME

BUILD A 'MAN CAVE' IN THE BASEMENT—WHICH IS REALLY JUST A ROOM FILLED WITH THE UGLY STUFF YOU CAN'T HAVE ANYWHERE ELSE.

- [ ] COMPLETED SUCCESSFULLY
- [ ] YET TO DO
- [ ] CERTIFIED EXPERT

SIGNED WITNESS

NOW GIVE IT A REVIEW

HOW MANY STARS?

☆ ☆ ☆ ☆ ☆

___ OUT OF FIVE

- [ ] HIGHLY RECOMMENDED
- [ ] IT WAS ENJOYABLE
- [ ] NOT WORTH THE TIME

WHEN ASKED A QUESTION THAT YOU DON'T KNOW THE ANSWER TO, DON'T BOTHER RESEARCHING IT—JUST MAKE SOMETHING UP.

COMPLETED SUCCESSFULLY ☐

YET TO DO ☐

CERTIFIED EXPERT ☐

SIGNED WITNESS

WITNESS REENACTMENT (SKETCH)

NOW GIVE IT A REVIEW

☐ HIGHLY RECOMMENDED

☐ IT WAS ENJOYABLE

☐ NOT WORTH THE TIME

HOW MANY STARS?

☆☆☆☆☆

___ OUT OF FIVE

ASK 'WHO LET THE CLEANING PERSON IN?' ANY TIME THE HOUSE IS SPOTLESS—BASICALLY CALLING YOUR SPOUSE A MAID.

- [ ] COMPLETED SUCCESSFULLY
- [ ] YET TO DO
- [ ] CERTIFIED EXPERT

SIGNED WITNESS

WITNESS REENACTMENT (SKETCH)

NOW GIVE IT A REVIEW

HOW MANY STARS?

☆☆☆☆☆

___ OUT OF FIVE

HIGHLY RECOMMENDED [ ]

IT WAS ENJOYABLE [ ]

NOT WORTH THE TIME [ ]

MANDATORY DAD CLICHÉ • NO. 198

REFER TO YOUR CHILDREN AS 'THE FRUIT OF MY LOINS.' IN PUBLIC.

SIGNED WITNESS

COMPLETED SUCCESSFULLY ☐

YET TO DO ☐

CERTIFIED EXPERT ☐

NOW GIVE IT A REVIEW

☐ HIGHLY RECOMMENDED

☐ IT WAS ENJOYABLE

☐ NOT WORTH THE TIME

HOW MANY STARS?

☆☆☆☆☆

___ OUT OF FIVE

MANDATORY DAD CLICHÉ • NO. 199

PASSIVELY AGGRESSIVELY COMMENT THAT YOUR KIDS NEVER CALL YOU ANYMORE – TO YOUR KIDS – THAT YOU JUST TALKED TO LAST WEEK.

SIGNED WITNESS

COMPLETED SUCCESSFULLY ☐

YET TO DO ☐

CERTIFIED EXPERT ☐

NOW GIVE IT A REVIEW

☐ HIGHLY RECOMMENDED

☐ IT WAS ENJOYABLE

☐ NOT WORTH THE TIME

HOW MANY STARS?

☆☆☆☆☆

___ OUT OF FIVE

WHEN SHOPPING FOR PECANS AT THE GROCERY STORE, BE SURE TO ASK YOUR KID TO GO GRAB A NUT SACK.

- ☐ COMPLETED SUCCESSFULLY
- ☐ YET TO DO
- ☐ CERTIFIED EXPERT

SIGNED WITNESS

'DAD, I'M HUNGRY' – 'HI HUNGRY, I'M DAD'. 'ARE YOU SERIOUS?' – 'NOPE, STILL DAD.'

- ☐ COMPLETED SUCCESSFULLY
- ☐ YET TO DO
- ☐ CERTIFIED EXPERT

SIGNED WITNESS

ENCOURAGE A FRIEND DEALING WITH THEIR OWN KID, WHILE THINKING 'MINE'S NO GENIUS, BUT AT LEAST THEY'RE NOT THAT DUMB.'

- ☐ COMPLETED SUCCESSFULLY
- ☐ YET TO DO
- ☐ CERTIFIED EXPERT

SIGNED WITNESS

MANDATORY DAD CLICHÉ • NO. 203

BEFORE A VACATION, CAREFULLY CULTIVATE
YOUR TAN LINES BY WEARING LARGE WATCHES,
T-SHIRTS, AND TUBE SOCKS WHEN OUTDOORS.

SIGNED WITNESS

COMPLETED SUCCESSFULLY ☐

YET TO DO ☐

CERTIFIED EXPERT ☐

NOW GIVE IT A REVIEW

☐ HIGHLY RECOMMENDED

☐ IT WAS ENJOYABLE

☐ NOT WORTH THE TIME

HOW MANY STARS?

☆ ☆ ☆ ☆ ☆

____ OUT OF FIVE

MANDATORY DAD CLICHÉ • NO. 204

FIND ANY EXCUSE TO USE YOUR POCKET KNIFE,
EVEN IF BETTER TOOLS ARE ON HAND. BOTTLE
OPENER? PASS, I'LL JUST PRY IT OFF W/ THIS.

SIGNED WITNESS

COMPLETED SUCCESSFULLY ☐

YET TO DO ☐

CERTIFIED EXPERT ☐

NOW GIVE IT A REVIEW

☐ HIGHLY RECOMMENDED

☐ IT WAS ENJOYABLE

☐ NOT WORTH THE TIME

HOW MANY STARS?

☆ ☆ ☆ ☆ ☆

____ OUT OF FIVE

SHOUT THAT YOU'RE 'NOT HEATING THE WHOLE NEIGHBORHOOD' ANYTIME SOMEONE HAS A DOOR OPEN FOR LONGER THAN 5 SECONDS.

- [ ] COMPLETED SUCCESSFULLY
- [ ] YET TO DO
- [ ] CERTIFIED EXPERT

SIGNED WITNESS

NOW GIVE IT A REVIEW

HOW MANY STARS?
☆☆☆☆☆
___ OUT OF FIVE

HIGHLY RECOMMENDED [ ]
IT WAS ENJOYABLE [ ]
NOT WORTH THE TIME [ ]

ACCIDENTALLY DROP YOUR KID. A LOT. LIKE, TO THE POINT THAT PEOPLE ARE STARTING TO ASK QUESTIONS.

- [ ] COMPLETED SUCCESSFULLY
- [ ] YET TO DO
- [ ] CERTIFIED EXPERT

SIGNED WITNESS

NOW GIVE IT A REVIEW

HOW MANY STARS?
☆☆☆☆☆
___ OUT OF FIVE

HIGHLY RECOMMENDED [ ]
IT WAS ENJOYABLE [ ]
NOT WORTH THE TIME [ ]

LOOK FORWARD TO, AND ACTUALLY ENJOY, MOWING THE GRASS—LIKE SOME KIND OF PSYCHOPATH.

	COMPLETED SUCCESSFULLY ☐
	YET TO DO ☐
	CERTIFIED EXPERT ☐
SIGNED WITNESS	

WITNESS REENACTMENT (SKETCH)

NOW GIVE IT A REVIEW

☐ HIGHLY RECOMMENDED

☐ IT WAS ENJOYABLE

☐ NOT WORTH THE TIME

HOW MANY STARS?

☆☆☆☆☆

_____ OUT OF FIVE

TELL PEOPLE THAT YOU NO LONGER PRACTICE YOUR OCCUPATION — BECAUSE YOU'RE SO GOOD, YOU DON'T NEED TO PRACTICE.

- ☐ COMPLETED SUCCESSFULLY
- ☐ YET TO DO
- ☐ CERTIFIED EXPERT

SIGNED WITNESS

WITNESS REENACTMENT (SKETCH)

NOW GIVE IT A REVIEW

HOW MANY STARS?

☆☆☆☆☆

—— OUT OF FIVE

HIGHLY RECOMMENDED ☐

IT WAS ENJOYABLE ☐

NOT WORTH THE TIME ☐

MANDATORY DAD CLICHÉ · NO. 209

REFER TO THE ENTIRE INTERNET AS 'YAHOO.'

SIGNED WITNESS

COMPLETED SUCCESSFULLY ☐

YET TO DO ☐

CERTIFIED EXPERT ☐

NOW GIVE IT A REVIEW

☐ HIGHLY RECOMMENDED

☐ IT WAS ENJOYABLE

☐ NOT WORTH THE TIME

HOW MANY STARS?

☆ ☆ ☆ ☆ ☆

___ OUT OF FIVE

MANDATORY DAD CLICHÉ · NO. 210

BURY YOUR KIDS IN THE SAND AT THE BEACH. NOW PRETEND TO WALK AWAY & END UP MAKING THEM CRY. FUN!

SIGNED WITNESS

COMPLETED SUCCESSFULLY ☐

YET TO DO ☐

CERTIFIED EXPERT ☐

NOW GIVE IT A REVIEW

☐ HIGHLY RECOMMENDED

☐ IT WAS ENJOYABLE

☐ NOT WORTH THE TIME

HOW MANY STARS?

☆ ☆ ☆ ☆ ☆

___ OUT OF FIVE

MANDATORY DAD CLICHÉ · NO. 211

PULL THE TRIGGER ON THAT POWER DRILL A FEW TIMES WHEN YOU PICK IT UP—JUST TO MAKE SURE IT'S STILL WORKING.

☐ COMPLETED SUCCESSFULLY

☐ YET TO DO

☐ CERTIFIED EXPERT

SIGNED WITNESS

NOW GIVE IT A REVIEW

HOW MANY STARS?

☆☆☆☆☆

___ OUT OF FIVE

HIGHLY RECOMMENDED ☐

IT WAS ENJOYABLE ☐

NOT WORTH THE TIME ☐

MANDATORY DAD CLICHÉ · NO. 212

SOMEHOW NEED TO TAKE YOUR GLASSES OFF ANY TIME YOU ASK SOMEONE TO REPEAT THEMSELVES.

☐ COMPLETED SUCCESSFULLY

☐ YET TO DO

☐ CERTIFIED EXPERT

SIGNED WITNESS

NOW GIVE IT A REVIEW

HOW MANY STARS?

☆☆☆☆☆

___ OUT OF FIVE

HIGHLY RECOMMENDED ☐

IT WAS ENJOYABLE ☐

NOT WORTH THE TIME ☐

MANDATORY DAD CLICHÉ · NO. 213

LIVE VICARIOUSLY THROUGH YOUR CHILD BY PUTTING THEM IN LITTLE LEAGUE—WHICH WILL BE FUN FOR THEM AFTER YOU GET KICKED OUT.

COMPLETED SUCCESSFULLY ☐

YET TO DO ☐

CERTIFIED EXPERT ☐

SIGNED WITNESS

MANDATORY DAD CLICHÉ · NO. 214

DRINK AT LEAST 10 CUPS OF COFFEE A DAY. PREFERABLY STALE AND BURNT, BUT ANYTHING WILL DO REALLY.

COMPLETED SUCCESSFULLY ☐

YET TO DO ☐

CERTIFIED EXPERT ☐

SIGNED WITNESS

MANDATORY DAD CLICHÉ · NO. 215

WAKE YOUR KID UP EARLY ON THE WEEKEND SO YOU CAN SPEND THE DAY TOGETHER—RUN OUT OF THINGS TO DO BY 10:30 A.M.

COMPLETED SUCCESSFULLY ☐

YET TO DO ☐

CERTIFIED EXPERT ☐

SIGNED WITNESS

ASK 'DO I INTERRUPT YOU WHEN YOU TALK?' IF YOUR KID CUTS YOU OFF. ALSO, OF COURSE YOU DO — THEY JUST BETTER NOT SAY THAT.

- [ ] COMPLETED SUCCESSFULLY
- [ ] YET TO DO
- [ ] CERTIFIED EXPERT

SIGNED WITNESS

WITNESS REENACTMENT (SKETCH)

NOW GIVE IT A REVIEW

HOW MANY STARS?

☆ ☆ ☆ ☆ ☆

___ OUT OF FIVE

HIGHLY RECOMMENDED [ ]

IT WAS ENJOYABLE [ ]

NOT WORTH THE TIME [ ]

HAVE ABSOLUTELY NO IDEA WHAT YOU GOT YOUR KIDS FOR CHRISTMAS UNTIL THEY OPEN THE GIFTS IN FRONT OF YOU.

COMPLETED SUCCESSFULLY ☐

YET TO DO ☐

CERTIFIED EXPERT ☐

SIGNED WITNESS

WITNESS REENACTMENT (SKETCH)

NOW GIVE IT A REVIEW

☐ HIGHLY RECOMMENDED

☐ IT WAS ENJOYABLE

☐ NOT WORTH THE TIME

HOW MANY STARS?

☆ ☆ ☆ ☆ ☆

___ OUT OF FIVE

EXPLAIN THAT DOING THINGS THAT YOU DON'T LIKE 'BUILDS CHARACTER.' JUST TRY TO SAY IT WITH A STRAIGHT FACE.

- [ ] COMPLETED SUCCESSFULLY
- [ ] YET TO DO
- [ ] CERTIFIED EXPERT

SIGNED WITNESS

NOW GIVE IT A REVIEW

HOW MANY STARS?

☆☆☆☆☆

___ OUT OF FIVE

HIGHLY RECOMMENDED [ ]

IT WAS ENJOYABLE [ ]

NOT WORTH THE TIME [ ]

YELL 'HOW IS IT POSSIBLE FOR THINGS TO GET SO DAMN TANGLED?!' WHILE PULLING OUT THE HOLIDAY LIGHTS YOU PUT AWAY LAST YEAR.

- [ ] COMPLETED SUCCESSFULLY
- [ ] YET TO DO
- [ ] CERTIFIED EXPERT

SIGNED WITNESS

NOW GIVE IT A REVIEW

HOW MANY STARS?

☆☆☆☆☆

___ OUT OF FIVE

HIGHLY RECOMMENDED [ ]

IT WAS ENJOYABLE [ ]

NOT WORTH THE TIME [ ]

ASSIGN YOUR KIDS CHORES.
IN OTHER WORDS, TASKS THAT YOU'LL HAVE
TO RE-DO AFTER THEY GO TO BED.

COMPLETED SUCCESSFULLY ☐

YET TO DO ☐

SIGNED WITNESS

CERTIFIED EXPERT ☐

WITNESS REENACTMENT (SKETCH)

NOW GIVE IT A REVIEW

☐ HIGHLY RECOMMENDED

☐ IT WAS ENJOYABLE

☐ NOT WORTH THE TIME

HOW MANY STARS?

☆ ☆ ☆ ☆ ☆

____ OUT OF FIVE

MANDATORY DAD CLICHÉ • NO. 221

CONSTANTLY COMPLAIN THAT 'I GUESS I HAVE TO DO EVERYTHING MYSELF AROUND HERE' WHILE NEVER LETTING ANYBODY HELP WITH ANYTHING.

☐ COMPLETED SUCCESSFULLY

☐ YET TO DO

☐ CERTIFIED EXPERT

SIGNED WITNESS

MANDATORY DAD CLICHÉ • NO. 222

FOR ONE MONTH STRAIGHT, CONSTANTLY DISCUSS AND EVALUATE THE IDEA OF BUYING A BOAT—THEN NEVER TALK ABOUT IT AGAIN.

☐ COMPLETED SUCCESSFULLY

☐ YET TO DO

☐ CERTIFIED EXPERT

SIGNED WITNESS

MANDATORY DAD CLICHÉ • NO. 223

THREATEN YOUR ENTIRE FAMILY WITH 'WE'RE ON VACATION & WE'RE GOING TO HAVE FUN!' LEAVE THE 'OR ELSE' PART SILENT.

☐ COMPLETED SUCCESSFULLY

☐ YET TO DO

☐ CERTIFIED EXPERT

SIGNED WITNESS

PERPETUALLY THINK THAT YOU'RE TWENTY YEARS YOUNGER THAN YOU ACTUALLY ARE—AND BACK IT UP WITH YOUR MATURITY LEVEL.

SIGNED WITNESS

COMPLETED SUCCESSFULLY ☐

YET TO DO ☐

CERTIFIED EXPERT ☐

NOW GIVE IT A REVIEW

☐ HIGHLY RECOMMENDED

☐ IT WAS ENJOYABLE

☐ NOT WORTH THE TIME

HOW MANY STARS?

☆☆☆☆☆

___ OUT OF FIVE

SAY 'WELL, I GUESS IT'S FREE THEN' WHEN SOMETHING DOESN'T SCAN AT THE REGISTER & SINGLE-HANDEDLY RUIN THAT CASHIER'S DAY.

SIGNED WITNESS

COMPLETED SUCCESSFULLY ☐

YET TO DO ☐

CERTIFIED EXPERT ☐

NOW GIVE IT A REVIEW

☐ HIGHLY RECOMMENDED

☐ IT WAS ENJOYABLE

☐ NOT WORTH THE TIME

HOW MANY STARS?

☆☆☆☆☆

___ OUT OF FIVE

IF YOUR KID DECIDES TO SIT ANYWHERE ELSE OTHER THAN RIGHT NEXT TO YOU, SAY 'WHAT, DO I SMELL OR SOMETHING?'

☐ COMPLETED SUCCESSFULLY

☐ YET TO DO

☐ CERTIFIED EXPERT

SIGNED WITNESS

NOW GIVE IT A REVIEW

HOW MANY STARS?

☆ ☆ ☆ ☆ ☆

___ OUT OF FIVE

HIGHLY RECOMMENDED ☐

IT WAS ENJOYABLE ☐

NOT WORTH THE TIME ☐

CONSTANTLY BRAG ABOUT BEING THE FIRST PERSON AWAKE ON VACATION—RIGHT UP UNTIL YOU FALL ASLEEP AT 3 PM.

☐ COMPLETED SUCCESSFULLY

☐ YET TO DO

☐ CERTIFIED EXPERT

SIGNED WITNESS

NOW GIVE IT A REVIEW

HOW MANY STARS?

☆ ☆ ☆ ☆ ☆

___ OUT OF FIVE

HIGHLY RECOMMENDED ☐

IT WAS ENJOYABLE ☐

NOT WORTH THE TIME ☐

RECEIVE A CHAIN EMAIL FROM AN OLD FRIEND & LAUGH AT HOW DUMB THEY ARE — BEFORE FORWARDING IT TO TEN PEOPLE JUST IN CASE.

SIGNED WITNESS

COMPLETED SUCCESSFULLY ☐

YET TO DO ☐

CERTIFIED EXPERT ☐

WITNESS REENACTMENT (SKETCH)

NOW GIVE IT A REVIEW

☐ HIGHLY RECOMMENDED

☐ IT WAS ENJOYABLE

☐ NOT WORTH THE TIME

HOW MANY STARS?

☆☆☆☆☆

___ OUT OF FIVE

MANDATORY DAD CLICHÉ · NO. 229

SAY SOMETHING LIKE 'OH, IT'S JUST ANOTHER DAY IN PARADISE' WHEN A CO-WORKER ASKS HOW YOU'RE DOING.

- [ ] COMPLETED SUCCESSFULLY
- [ ] YET TO DO
- [ ] CERTIFIED EXPERT

SIGNED WITNESS

WITNESS REENACTMENT (SKETCH)

NOW GIVE IT A REVIEW

HOW MANY STARS?

☆☆☆☆☆

___ OUT OF FIVE

- [ ] HIGHLY RECOMMENDED
- [ ] IT WAS ENJOYABLE
- [ ] NOT WORTH THE TIME

SUDDENLY DECIDE TO EITHER GROW OR SHAVE A MUSTACHE—CAUSING EVERY PERSON YOU KNOW TO BEG YOU TO STOP.

SIGNED WITNESS

COMPLETED SUCCESSFULLY ☐

YET TO DO ☐

CERTIFIED EXPERT ☐

WITNESS REENACTMENT (SKETCH)

NOW GIVE IT A REVIEW

☐ HIGHLY RECOMMENDED

☐ IT WAS ENJOYABLE

☐ NOT WORTH THE TIME

HOW MANY STARS?

☆ ☆ ☆ ☆ ☆

___ OUT OF FIVE

MANDATORY DAD CLICHÉ • NO. 231

SAY SOMETHING LIKE 'IT'S A BIT NIPPLEY OUT TODAY' WHEN IT'S COLD, DESPITE EVERYONE TELLING YOU THAT YOU CAN'T SAY THAT.

☐ COMPLETED SUCCESSFULLY

☐ YET TO DO

☐ CERTIFIED EXPERT

SIGNED WITNESS

MANDATORY DAD CLICHÉ • NO. 232

SPEND AN ENTIRE WEEKEND CLEANING THE GARAGE—AND THE NEXT 2 MONTHS BITCHING THAT YOU CAN'T FIND ANYTHING.

☐ COMPLETED SUCCESSFULLY

☐ YET TO DO

☐ CERTIFIED EXPERT

SIGNED WITNESS

MANDATORY DAD CLICHÉ • NO. 233

BE PHYSICALLY UNABLE TO WRAP GIFTS IN AN AESTHETICALLY PLEASING MANNER—OFTEN FORGETTING THAT BOXES EVEN EXIST.

☐ COMPLETED SUCCESSFULLY

☐ YET TO DO

☐ CERTIFIED EXPERT

SIGNED WITNESS

TELL YOUR KIDS TO ASK THEIR MOTHER—WHEN YOU KNOW FULL WELL THAT THEY DON'T STAND A CHANCE.

SIGNED WITNESS

COMPLETED SUCCESSFULLY ☐

YET TO DO ☐

CERTIFIED EXPERT ☐

WITNESS REENACTMENT (SKETCH)

NOW GIVE IT A REVIEW

☐ HIGHLY RECOMMENDED

☐ IT WAS ENJOYABLE

☐ NOT WORTH THE TIME

HOW MANY STARS?

☆ ☆ ☆ ☆ ☆

___ OUT OF FIVE

BE THE DESIGNATED PIGGYBACK RIDE GIVER, WHILE PRAYING THAT THEY OUTGROW IT BEFORE THEY SEND YOU TO THE HOSPITAL.

- [ ] COMPLETED SUCCESSFULLY
- [ ] YET TO DO
- [ ] CERTIFIED EXPERT

SIGNED WITNESS

WITNESS REENACTMENT (SKETCH)

NOW GIVE IT A REVIEW

HOW MANY STARS?

☆ ☆ ☆ ☆ ☆

___ OUT OF FIVE

- [ ] HIGHLY RECOMMENDED
- [ ] IT WAS ENJOYABLE
- [ ] NOT WORTH THE TIME

HIDE THE EASTER EGGS. ALSO, FORGET WHERE YOU HID SAID EASTER EGGS—UNTIL THE SMELL ULTIMATELY GIVES AWAY THEIR LOCATIONS.

SIGNED WITNESS

COMPLETED SUCCESSFULLY ☐

YET TO DO ☐

CERTIFIED EXPERT ☐

NOW GIVE IT A REVIEW

☐ HIGHLY RECOMMENDED

☐ IT WAS ENJOYABLE

☐ NOT WORTH THE TIME

HOW MANY STARS?

☆ ☆ ☆ ☆ ☆

___ OUT OF FIVE

TELL YOUR KIDS 'NOT TO LET THE BED BUGS BITE' AS YOU TUCK THEM IN...IN THE MOST TERRIFYING WAY POSSIBLE.

SIGNED WITNESS

COMPLETED SUCCESSFULLY ☐

YET TO DO ☐

CERTIFIED EXPERT ☐

NOW GIVE IT A REVIEW

☐ HIGHLY RECOMMENDED

☐ IT WAS ENJOYABLE

☐ NOT WORTH THE TIME

HOW MANY STARS?

☆ ☆ ☆ ☆ ☆

___ OUT OF FIVE

PERFECT THE ART OF JUST SILENTLY STARING AT YOUR KID UNTIL THEY START BEHAVING.

☐ COMPLETED SUCCESSFULLY

☐ YET TO DO

☐ CERTIFIED EXPERT

SIGNED WITNESS

NOW GIVE IT A REVIEW

HOW MANY STARS?

☆ ☆ ☆ ☆ ☆

—— OUT OF FIVE

HIGHLY RECOMMENDED ☐

IT WAS ENJOYABLE ☐

NOT WORTH THE TIME ☐

TELL YOUR KID TO 'PUT A SWEATER ON IF YOU'RE COLD' AS YOU KEEP THE HOUSE AT A COZY FIFTY-FOUR DEGREES IN THE WINTER.

☐ COMPLETED SUCCESSFULLY

☐ YET TO DO

☐ CERTIFIED EXPERT

SIGNED WITNESS

NOW GIVE IT A REVIEW

HOW MANY STARS?

☆ ☆ ☆ ☆ ☆

—— OUT OF FIVE

HIGHLY RECOMMENDED ☐

IT WAS ENJOYABLE ☐

NOT WORTH THE TIME ☐

START THE GAME OF THROWING YOUR KIDS AS
FAR AS YOU CAN INTO POOLS, BECAUSE IT'S THE
ONLY TIME YOU'RE ALLOWED TO THROW THEM.

COMPLETED SUCCESSFULLY ☐

YET TO DO ☐

CERTIFIED EXPERT ☐

SIGNED WITNESS

WITNESS REENACTMENT (SKETCH)

NOW GIVE IT A REVIEW

☐ HIGHLY RECOMMENDED

☐ IT WAS ENJOYABLE

☐ NOT WORTH THE TIME

HOW MANY STARS?

☆ ☆ ☆ ☆ ☆

___ OUT OF FIVE

AGREE TO LET YOUR KIDS EAT NOTHING BUT JUNK FOOD FOR DINNER–UNDER THE CONDITION OF 'DON'T TELL MOM.'

☐ COMPLETED SUCCESSFULLY

☐ YET TO DO

☐ CERTIFIED EXPERT

SIGNED WITNESS

WITNESS REENACTMENT (SKETCH)

NOW GIVE IT A REVIEW

HOW MANY STARS?

☆☆☆☆☆

___ OUT OF FIVE

HIGHLY RECOMMENDED ☐

IT WAS ENJOYABLE ☐

NOT WORTH THE TIME ☐

MANDATORY DAD CLICHÉ • NO. 242

INSIST ON LEAVING YOUR KID A VOICEMAIL
IF THEY DON'T ANSWER—INCLUDE USEFUL INFO
LIKE 'HEY, IT'S YOUR DAD. CALL ME BACK.'

SIGNED WITNESS

COMPLETED SUCCESSFULLY ☐

YET TO DO ☐

CERTIFIED EXPERT ☐

MANDATORY DAD CLICHÉ • NO. 243

WATCHING A VIDEO ON YOUR PHONE IN
A PUBLIC PLACE? MAKE SURE IT'S SET TO FULL
VOLUME—AND PLAY THE WHOLE THING.

SIGNED WITNESS

COMPLETED SUCCESSFULLY ☐

YET TO DO ☐

CERTIFIED EXPERT ☐

MANDATORY DAD CLICHÉ • NO. 244

IF YOUR CHILD EATS THEIR WHOLE MEAL,
SAY SOMETHING LIKE 'WELL, I'M SORRY THAT
YOU DIDN'T LIKE IT.

SIGNED WITNESS

COMPLETED SUCCESSFULLY ☐

YET TO DO ☐

CERTIFIED EXPERT ☐

TELL YOUR SIXTEEN-YEAR-OLD THAT THEIR BIRTHDAY PRESENT IS IN THE DRIVEWAY—WHERE YOU PLACED A BRAND NEW MATCHBOX CAR.

☐ COMPLETED SUCCESSFULLY

☐ YET TO DO

☐ CERTIFIED EXPERT

SIGNED WITNESS

NOW GIVE IT A REVIEW

HOW MANY STARS?
☆ ☆ ☆ ☆ ☆
___ OUT OF FIVE

HIGHLY RECOMMENDED ☐

IT WAS ENJOYABLE ☐

NOT WORTH THE TIME ☐

SAY THINGS LIKE 'WHEN I WAS YOUR AGE, I HAD TO WALK TO SCHOOL' BECAUSE THEY HAVE ABSOLUTELY NO WAY TO PROVE YOU'RE LYING.

☐ COMPLETED SUCCESSFULLY

☐ YET TO DO

☐ CERTIFIED EXPERT

SIGNED WITNESS

NOW GIVE IT A REVIEW

HOW MANY STARS?
☆ ☆ ☆ ☆ ☆
___ OUT OF FIVE

HIGHLY RECOMMENDED ☐

IT WAS ENJOYABLE ☐

NOT WORTH THE TIME ☐

NEED TO READ SOMETHING SMALL? RAPIDLY ALTERNATE HOLDING IT AS CLOSE & AS FAR AWAY AS POSSIBLE – AND BE SURE TO SQUINT.

SIGNED WITNESS

COMPLETED SUCCESSFULLY ☐

YET TO DO ☐

CERTIFIED EXPERT ☐

WITNESS REENACTMENT (SKETCH)

NOW GIVE IT A REVIEW

☐ HIGHLY RECOMMENDED

☐ IT WAS ENJOYABLE

☐ NOT WORTH THE TIME

HOW MANY STARS?

☆☆☆☆☆

____ OUT OF FIVE

DESIGNATE A SPECIFIC CHAIR THAT ONLY YOU ARE ALLOWED TO SIT IN, DESPITE THE FACT THAT YOU HARDLY EVER SIT DOWN IN IT.

☐ COMPLETED SUCCESSFULLY

☐ YET TO DO

☐ CERTIFIED EXPERT

SIGNED WITNESS

WITNESS REENACTMENT (SKETCH)

NOW GIVE IT A REVIEW

HOW MANY STARS?

☆☆☆☆☆

—— OUT OF FIVE

HIGHLY RECOMMENDED ☐

IT WAS ENJOYABLE ☐

NOT WORTH THE TIME ☐

MANDATORY DAD CLICHÉ • NO. 249

ONLY OWN SHORTS THAT HAVE AT LEAST TWENTY POCKETS—AT AN ABSOLUTE MINIMUM.

SIGNED WITNESS

COMPLETED SUCCESSFULLY ☐

YET TO DO ☐

CERTIFIED EXPERT ☐

NOW GIVE IT A REVIEW

☐ HIGHLY RECOMMENDED

☐ IT WAS ENJOYABLE

☐ NOT WORTH THE TIME

HOW MANY STARS?

☆ ☆ ☆ ☆ ☆

___ OUT OF FIVE

MANDATORY DAD CLICHÉ • NO. 250

HELP YOUR KIDS WITH THEIR HOMEWORK BY TELLING THEM THAT THE TEACHER IS DOING IT WRONG—SO YOU CAN'T REALLY HELP THEM.

SIGNED WITNESS

COMPLETED SUCCESSFULLY ☐

YET TO DO ☐

CERTIFIED EXPERT ☐

NOW GIVE IT A REVIEW

☐ HIGHLY RECOMMENDED

☐ IT WAS ENJOYABLE

☐ NOT WORTH THE TIME

HOW MANY STARS?

☆ ☆ ☆ ☆ ☆

___ OUT OF FIVE

BUY YOUR KIDS GIFTS THAT ARE REALLY JUST
THINGS THAT YOU WANTED WHEN YOU WERE
A KID—LIKE THAT SUPER COOL ROCK TUMBLER.

☐ COMPLETED SUCCESSFULLY

☐ YET TO DO

☐ CERTIFIED EXPERT

SIGNED WITNESS

NOW GIVE IT A REVIEW

HOW MANY STARS?

☆ ☆ ☆ ☆ ☆

___ OUT OF FIVE

HIGHLY RECOMMENDED ☐

IT WAS ENJOYABLE ☐

NOT WORTH THE TIME ☐

SETTLE ALL SIBLING DISPUTES BY
JUST EATING WHATEVER FOOD IT IS THAT
THEY'RE FIGHTING ABOUT.

☐ COMPLETED SUCCESSFULLY

☐ YET TO DO

☐ CERTIFIED EXPERT

SIGNED WITNESS

NOW GIVE IT A REVIEW

HOW MANY STARS?

☆ ☆ ☆ ☆ ☆

___ OUT OF FIVE

HIGHLY RECOMMENDED ☐

IT WAS ENJOYABLE ☐

NOT WORTH THE TIME ☐

DECLARE ANYBODY THAT'S DRIVING FIVE MILES AN HOUR FASTER OR SLOWER THAN YOU A 'LUNATIC.'

SIGNED WITNESS

COMPLETED SUCCESSFULLY ☐

YET TO DO ☐

CERTIFIED EXPERT ☐

WITNESS REENACTMENT (SKETCH)

NOW GIVE IT A REVIEW

☐ HIGHLY RECOMMENDED

☐ IT WAS ENJOYABLE

☐ NOT WORTH THE TIME

HOW MANY STARS?

☆☆☆☆☆

___ OUT OF FIVE

MANDATORY DAD CLICHÉ · NO. 254

WHENEVER USING A STUD FINDER, POINT IT AT YOURSELF & MAKE A BEEPING NOISE – FOLLOW IT UP WITH 'FOUND ONE' TO SEAL THE DEAL.

- [ ] COMPLETED SUCCESSFULLY
- [ ] YET TO DO
- [ ] CERTIFIED EXPERT

SIGNED WITNESS

WITNESS REENACTMENT (SKETCH)

NOW GIVE IT A REVIEW

HOW MANY STARS?

☆☆☆☆☆

____ OUT OF FIVE

HIGHLY RECOMMENDED [ ]

IT WAS ENJOYABLE [ ]

NOT WORTH THE TIME [ ]

MANDATORY DAD CLICHÉ • NO. 255

TELL EVERYBODY, EVEN RANDOM PEOPLE ON THE STREET, WHEN YOU HEAR THAT IT MIGHT BE IN THE SIXTIES NEXT WEEK.

SIGNED WITNESS

COMPLETED SUCCESSFULLY ☐

YET TO DO ☐

CERTIFIED EXPERT ☐

NOW GIVE IT A REVIEW

☐ HIGHLY RECOMMENDED

☐ IT WAS ENJOYABLE

☐ NOT WORTH THE TIME

HOW MANY STARS?

☆ ☆ ☆ ☆ ☆

___ OUT OF FIVE

MANDATORY DAD CLICHÉ • NO. 256

SAY 'THEY CALL THIS MUSIC?' ABOUT ANY SONG PRODUCED AFTER THE YEAR YOU GRADUATED FROM HIGH SCHOOL.

SIGNED WITNESS

COMPLETED SUCCESSFULLY ☐

YET TO DO ☐

CERTIFIED EXPERT ☐

NOW GIVE IT A REVIEW

☐ HIGHLY RECOMMENDED

☐ IT WAS ENJOYABLE

☐ NOT WORTH THE TIME

HOW MANY STARS?

☆ ☆ ☆ ☆ ☆

___ OUT OF FIVE

ON A VACATION? BETTER FLIP TO THE WEATHER CHANNEL IN THE HOTEL ROOM—AND KEEP IT ON ALL DAY.

- [ ] COMPLETED SUCCESSFULLY
- [ ] YET TO DO
- [ ] CERTIFIED EXPERT

SIGNED WITNESS

NOW GIVE IT A REVIEW

HOW MANY STARS?

☆ ☆ ☆ ☆ ☆

—— OUT OF FIVE

- HIGHLY RECOMMENDED [ ]
- IT WAS ENJOYABLE [ ]
- NOT WORTH THE TIME [ ]

ROLL DOWN YOUR CAR WINDOW AND SHOUT 'HEY THERE!' WHENEVER DRIVING BY A FIELD OF HAY BALES.

- [ ] COMPLETED SUCCESSFULLY
- [ ] YET TO DO
- [ ] CERTIFIED EXPERT

SIGNED WITNESS

NOW GIVE IT A REVIEW

HOW MANY STARS?

☆ ☆ ☆ ☆ ☆

—— OUT OF FIVE

- HIGHLY RECOMMENDED [ ]
- IT WAS ENJOYABLE [ ]
- NOT WORTH THE TIME [ ]

MANDATORY DAD CLICHÉ • NO. 259

IF YOUR CHILD SPENDS MORE THAN 2 MINUTES USING THE RESTROOM, KNOCK ON THE DOOR & ASK THEM IF THEY FELL IN.

COMPLETED SUCCESSFULLY ☐

YET TO DO ☐

CERTIFIED EXPERT ☐

SIGNED WITNESS

MANDATORY DAD CLICHÉ • NO. 260

SAY SOMETHING LIKE 'WELL, I GUESS WE'RE GOING TO HAVE TO AMPUTATE' WHEN YOUR KID GETS A PAPER CUT.

COMPLETED SUCCESSFULLY ☐

YET TO DO ☐

CERTIFIED EXPERT ☐

SIGNED WITNESS

MANDATORY DAD CLICHÉ • NO. 261

TEACH YOUR KIDS IMPORTANT CAR SAFETY LESSONS—LIKE ALWAYS WEARING A SEATBELT & NEVER, EVER TURNING ON THE DOME LIGHT.

COMPLETED SUCCESSFULLY ☐

YET TO DO ☐

CERTIFIED EXPERT ☐

SIGNED WITNESS

WHEN WALKING OUT OF A RESTAURANT, GRAB A HANDFUL OF MINTS FROM THE BOWL AND SAY 'WELL I DON'T MIND IF I DO.'

- ☐ COMPLETED SUCCESSFULLY
- ☐ YET TO DO
- ☐ CERTIFIED EXPERT

SIGNED WITNESS

WITNESS REENACTMENT (SKETCH)

NOW GIVE IT A REVIEW

HOW MANY STARS?

☆☆☆☆☆

___ OUT OF FIVE

HIGHLY RECOMMENDED ☐

IT WAS ENJOYABLE ☐

NOT WORTH THE TIME ☐

TALK ABOUT HOW MUCH WE NEEDED THIS RAIN—LITERALLY EVERY SINGLE TIME THAT IT RAINS.

COMPLETED SUCCESSFULLY ☐

YET TO DO ☐

CERTIFIED EXPERT ☐

SIGNED WITNESS

WITNESS REENACTMENT (SKETCH)

NOW GIVE IT A REVIEW

☐ HIGHLY RECOMMENDED

☐ IT WAS ENJOYABLE

☐ NOT WORTH THE TIME

HOW MANY STARS?

☆☆☆☆☆

___ OUT OF FIVE

GO ON AND ON ABOUT HOW GREAT THE FOOD WAS AFTER EATING AT A TGI FRIDAYS.

☐ COMPLETED SUCCESSFULLY

☐ YET TO DO

☐ CERTIFIED EXPERT

SIGNED WITNESS

NOW GIVE IT A REVIEW

HOW MANY STARS?

☆ ☆ ☆ ☆ ☆

___ OUT OF FIVE

HIGHLY RECOMMENDED ☐

IT WAS ENJOYABLE ☐

NOT WORTH THE TIME ☐

TURN YOUR KID'S MISTAKE INTO A TEACHABLE MOMENT USING WISDOM LIKE 'I DON'T WANT TO SAY I TOLD YOU SO, BUT I TOLD YOU SO.'

☐ COMPLETED SUCCESSFULLY

☐ YET TO DO

☐ CERTIFIED EXPERT

SIGNED WITNESS

NOW GIVE IT A REVIEW

HOW MANY STARS?

☆ ☆ ☆ ☆ ☆

___ OUT OF FIVE

HIGHLY RECOMMENDED ☐

IT WAS ENJOYABLE ☐

NOT WORTH THE TIME ☐

SAY 'WHAT'S THIS WORLD COMING TO?' OUT LOUD AFTER SILENTLY READING ANY NEWS ARTICLE.

SIGNED WITNESS

COMPLETED SUCCESSFULLY ☐

YET TO DO ☐

CERTIFIED EXPERT ☐

WITNESS REENACTMENT (SKETCH)

NOW GIVE IT A REVIEW

☐ HIGHLY RECOMMENDED

☐ IT WAS ENJOYABLE

☐ NOT WORTH THE TIME

HOW MANY STARS?

☆☆☆☆☆

___ OUT OF FIVE

MANDATORY DAD CLICHÉ • NO. 267

SAY 'WOW, IT'S A GOOD THING THAT WE GOT HERE WHEN WE DID' WHEN PEOPLE KEEP GETTING BEHIND YOU IN ANY LINE.

☐ COMPLETED SUCCESSFULLY

☐ YET TO DO

☐ CERTIFIED EXPERT

SIGNED WITNESS

MANDATORY DAD CLICHÉ • NO. 268

CONSTANTLY TALK ABOUT HOW IT'S NOT REALLY THAT HOT OUT—JUST HUMID.

☐ COMPLETED SUCCESSFULLY

☐ YET TO DO

☐ CERTIFIED EXPERT

SIGNED WITNESS

MANDATORY DAD CLICHÉ • NO. 269

EXPLAIN THE DANGERS OF HAVING UNPROTECTED SEX TO YOUR CHILDREN—BY SHOWING THEM PHOTOS OF THEMSELVES.

☐ COMPLETED SUCCESSFULLY

☐ YET TO DO

☐ CERTIFIED EXPERT

SIGNED WITNESS

KEEP THE FRIDGE STOCKED WITH THE BEST CHEAP DOMESTIC BEER THAT YOU CAN FIND ON SALE.

SIGNED WITNESS

COMPLETED SUCCESSFULLY ☐

YET TO DO ☐

CERTIFIED EXPERT ☐

NOW GIVE IT A REVIEW

☐ HIGHLY RECOMMENDED

☐ IT WAS ENJOYABLE

☐ NOT WORTH THE TIME

HOW MANY STARS?

☆☆☆☆☆

___ OUT OF FIVE

TELL YOUR KID 'WHEN YOU PAY THE RENT, YOU CAN MAKE THE RULES'—BUT MAINLY AS AN INCENTIVE TO GET THEM OUT OF YOUR HOUSE.

SIGNED WITNESS

COMPLETED SUCCESSFULLY ☐

YET TO DO ☐

CERTIFIED EXPERT ☐

NOW GIVE IT A REVIEW

☐ HIGHLY RECOMMENDED

☐ IT WAS ENJOYABLE

☐ NOT WORTH THE TIME

HOW MANY STARS?

☆☆☆☆☆

___ OUT OF FIVE

MANDATORY DAD CLICHÉ • NO. 272

LET YOUR KIDS HANDLE THEIR OWN PROBLEMS—BUT ALSO SECRETLY THREATEN TO MURDER ANYONE THAT UPSETS THEM.

- [ ] COMPLETED SUCCESSFULLY
- [ ] YET TO DO
- [ ] CERTIFIED EXPERT

SIGNED WITNESS

NOW GIVE IT A REVIEW

HOW MANY STARS?

☆ ☆ ☆ ☆ ☆

___ OUT OF FIVE

HIGHLY RECOMMENDED [ ]

IT WAS ENJOYABLE [ ]

NOT WORTH THE TIME [ ]

MANDATORY DAD CLICHÉ • NO. 273

SAY 'HOW MUCH!?' WHEN THE COST OF ANYTHING IS MORE THAN APPROXIMATELY THREE DOLLARS.

- [ ] COMPLETED SUCCESSFULLY
- [ ] YET TO DO
- [ ] CERTIFIED EXPERT

SIGNED WITNESS

NOW GIVE IT A REVIEW

HOW MANY STARS?

☆ ☆ ☆ ☆ ☆

___ OUT OF FIVE

HIGHLY RECOMMENDED [ ]

IT WAS ENJOYABLE [ ]

NOT WORTH THE TIME [ ]

MANDATORY DAD CLICHÉ · NO. 274

DON'T BOTHER WALKING AROUND A STORE TO LOOK FOR YOUR FAMILY—JUST WHISTLE AS LOUD AS HUMANLY POSSIBLE.

	COMPLETED SUCCESSFULLY ☐
	YET TO DO ☐
SIGNED WITNESS	CERTIFIED EXPERT ☐

WITNESS REENACTMENT (SKETCH)

NOW GIVE IT A REVIEW

☐ HIGHLY RECOMMENDED

☐ IT WAS ENJOYABLE

☐ NOT WORTH THE TIME

HOW MANY STARS?

☆☆☆☆☆

___ OUT OF FIVE

SAY 'STOP CRYING OR I'LL GIVE YA SOMETHING TO CRY ABOUT' TO THREATEN THEM WITH VIOLENCE IN THE MOST FUN WAY POSSIBLE.

- ☐ COMPLETED SUCCESSFULLY
- ☐ YET TO DO
- ☐ CERTIFIED EXPERT

SIGNED WITNESS

WITNESS REENACTMENT (SKETCH)

NOW GIVE IT A REVIEW

HOW MANY STARS?

☆☆☆☆☆

___ OUT OF FIVE

- HIGHLY RECOMMENDED ☐
- IT WAS ENJOYABLE ☐
- NOT WORTH THE TIME ☐

ASK YOUR KIDS IF THEY'RE GOING TO SLEEP ALL DAY—WHEN YOU STARTLE THEM AWAKE AT 6:45 AM.

SIGNED WITNESS

COMPLETED SUCCESSFULLY ☐

YET TO DO ☐

CERTIFIED EXPERT ☐

WITNESS REENACTMENT (SKETCH)

NOW GIVE IT A REVIEW

☐ HIGHLY RECOMMENDED

☐ IT WAS ENJOYABLE

☐ NOT WORTH THE TIME

HOW MANY STARS?

☆ ☆ ☆ ☆ ☆

___ OUT OF FIVE

MANDATORY DAD CLICHÉ • NO. 277

TURN TO YOUR KID AND SAY 'OPE, THEY'RE COMING FOR YOU' ANY TIME THAT YOU HEAR A SIREN.

☐ COMPLETED SUCCESSFULLY

☐ YET TO DO

☐ CERTIFIED EXPERT

SIGNED WITNESS

MANDATORY DAD CLICHÉ • NO. 278

GIVE SOMEBODY YOUR SHOPPING CART IN THE PARKING LOT—TELL THEM THAT YOU LEFT SOME GAS IN IT FOR THEM.

☐ COMPLETED SUCCESSFULLY

☐ YET TO DO

☐ CERTIFIED EXPERT

SIGNED WITNESS

MANDATORY DAD CLICHÉ • NO. 279

START CARRYING AROUND A CRUSTY HANDKERCHIEF INSTEAD OF JUST USING A KLEENEX LIKE A NORMAL HUMAN BEING.

☐ COMPLETED SUCCESSFULLY

☐ YET TO DO

☐ CERTIFIED EXPERT

SIGNED WITNESS

REFUSE TO PEEL THE PROTECTIVE PLASTIC FILM OFF ANY NEW ELECTRONICS.

SIGNED WITNESS

COMPLETED SUCCESSFULLY ☐

YET TO DO ☐

CERTIFIED EXPERT ☐

WITNESS REENACTMENT (SKETCH)

NOW GIVE IT A REVIEW

☐ HIGHLY RECOMMENDED

☐ IT WAS ENJOYABLE

☐ NOT WORTH THE TIME

HOW MANY STARS?
☆☆☆☆☆
___ OUT OF FIVE

SAY THINGS LIKE 'NOW DON'T GO SPENDING A LOT ON ME' DESPITE KNOWING THAT IT REALLY WASN'T GOING TO BE AN ISSUE ANYWAY.

☐ COMPLETED SUCCESSFULLY

☐ YET TO DO

☐ CERTIFIED EXPERT

SIGNED WITNESS

WITNESS REENACTMENT (SKETCH)

NOW GIVE IT A REVIEW

HOW MANY STARS?

☆ ☆ ☆ ☆ ☆

— OUT OF FIVE

HIGHLY RECOMMENDED ☐

IT WAS ENJOYABLE ☐

NOT WORTH THE TIME ☐

MANDATORY DAD CLICHÉ • NO. 282

SPEND 45 MINUTES LOOKING FOR YOUR READING GLASSES—THAT ARE ON TOP OF YOUR HEAD.

SIGNED WITNESS

COMPLETED SUCCESSFULLY ☐

YET TO DO ☐

CERTIFIED EXPERT ☐

NOW GIVE IT A REVIEW

☐ HIGHLY RECOMMENDED

☐ IT WAS ENJOYABLE

☐ NOT WORTH THE TIME

HOW MANY STARS?

☆ ☆ ☆ ☆ ☆

___ OUT OF FIVE

MANDATORY DAD CLICHÉ • NO. 283

GIVE YOUR KIDS SINCERE & THOUGHTFUL LIFE ADVICE THAT THEY WILL PROMPTLY DO THE EXACT OPPOSITE OF.

SIGNED WITNESS

COMPLETED SUCCESSFULLY ☐

YET TO DO ☐

CERTIFIED EXPERT ☐

NOW GIVE IT A REVIEW

☐ HIGHLY RECOMMENDED

☐ IT WAS ENJOYABLE

☐ NOT WORTH THE TIME

HOW MANY STARS?

☆ ☆ ☆ ☆ ☆

___ OUT OF FIVE

MANDATORY DAD CLICHÉ · NO. 284

ASK YOUR KID 'WHEN WAS THE LAST TIME YOU CHECKED YOUR OIL?' WHENEVER IT COMES TO MIND—LIKE DURING THEIR WEDDING VOWS.

- ☐ COMPLETED SUCCESSFULLY
- ☐ YET TO DO
- ☐ CERTIFIED EXPERT

SIGNED WITNESS

NOW GIVE IT A REVIEW

HOW MANY STARS?

☆ ☆ ☆ ☆ ☆

___ OUT OF FIVE

- HIGHLY RECOMMENDED ☐
- IT WAS ENJOYABLE ☐
- NOT WORTH THE TIME ☐

MANDATORY DAD CLICHÉ · NO. 285

GIVE THE BEST STOCKING STUFFERS—LIKE A BRAND NEW ICE SCRAPER FROM THE GAS STATION DOWN THE STREET.

- ☐ COMPLETED SUCCESSFULLY
- ☐ YET TO DO
- ☐ CERTIFIED EXPERT

SIGNED WITNESS

NOW GIVE IT A REVIEW

HOW MANY STARS?

☆ ☆ ☆ ☆ ☆

___ OUT OF FIVE

- HIGHLY RECOMMENDED ☐
- IT WAS ENJOYABLE ☐
- NOT WORTH THE TIME ☐

SPEND FIVE MINUTES PERFECTLY SIGNING YOUR NAME WITH YOUR FINGER ON EVERY IPAD CHECKOUT SCREEN.

SIGNED WITNESS

COMPLETED SUCCESSFULLY ☐

YET TO DO ☐

CERTIFIED EXPERT ☐

WITNESS REENACTMENT (SKETCH)

NOW GIVE IT A REVIEW

☐ HIGHLY RECOMMENDED

☐ IT WAS ENJOYABLE

☐ NOT WORTH THE TIME

HOW MANY STARS?

☆ ☆ ☆ ☆ ☆

___ OUT OF FIVE

SAY SOMETHING LIKE 'WELL LOOK WHO THE CAT DRAGGED IN' WHENEVER YOUR KID HAS BEEN GONE FOR OVER AN HOUR.

- ☐ COMPLETED SUCCESSFULLY
- ☐ YET TO DO
- ☐ CERTIFIED EXPERT

SIGNED WITNESS

WITNESS REENACTMENT (SKETCH)

NOW GIVE IT A REVIEW

HOW MANY STARS?

☆ ☆ ☆ ☆ ☆

— OUT OF FIVE

HIGHLY RECOMMENDED ☐

IT WAS ENJOYABLE ☐

NOT WORTH THE TIME ☐

MANDATORY DAD CLICHÉ • NO. 288

**START PACKING FOR A TWO WEEK
VACATION APPROXIMATELY 30 MINUTES
BEFORE HEADING TO THE AIRPORT.**

COMPLETED SUCCESSFULLY ☐

YET TO DO ☐

CERTIFIED EXPERT ☐

SIGNED WITNESS

MANDATORY DAD CLICHÉ • NO. 289

**BUY A SWEET, SENTIMENTAL CARD FOR
YOUR KID ON THEIR BIRTHDAY—BUT CROSS OUT
ANY ADJECTIVES THAT DON'T APPLY TO THEM.**

COMPLETED SUCCESSFULLY ☐

YET TO DO ☐

CERTIFIED EXPERT ☐

SIGNED WITNESS

MANDATORY DAD CLICHÉ • NO. 290

**PROCLAIM THAT 'VIDEO GAMES WILL ROT
YOUR BRAIN' WHILE WATCHING FOOTBALL FOR
18 STRAIGHT HOURS ON A SUNDAY.**

COMPLETED SUCCESSFULLY ☐

YET TO DO ☐

CERTIFIED EXPERT ☐

SIGNED WITNESS

TELL YOUR CHILD TO 'WASTE NOT, WANT NOT' AS YOU FORCE THEM TO RIP A PAPER TOWEL IN HALF BEFORE USING IT.

☐ COMPLETED SUCCESSFULLY

☐ YET TO DO

☐ CERTIFIED EXPERT

SIGNED WITNESS

NOW GIVE IT A REVIEW

HOW MANY STARS?

☆ ☆ ☆ ☆ ☆

___ OUT OF FIVE

HIGHLY RECOMMENDED ☐

IT WAS ENJOYABLE ☐

NOT WORTH THE TIME ☐

LOVE YOUR KIDS MORE THAN ANYTHING IN THE WORLD — DESPITE WHAT YOU TELL EVERYBODY ELSE.

☐ COMPLETED SUCCESSFULLY

☐ YET TO DO

☐ CERTIFIED EXPERT

SIGNED WITNESS

NOW GIVE IT A REVIEW

HOW MANY STARS?

☆ ☆ ☆ ☆ ☆

___ OUT OF FIVE

HIGHLY RECOMMENDED ☐

IT WAS ENJOYABLE ☐

NOT WORTH THE TIME ☐

WRITE DOWN THE THINGS THAT YOUR DAD WAS NOTORIOUS FOR DOING. NOW TORMENT YOUR OWN KIDS WITH THEM.

DON'T STOP WITH ONE. USE THE NEXT FEW PAGES TOO.

— NO PAPER? WELL, YOU'RE IN LUCK. —

MANDATORY DAD CLICHÉ · LIKE FATHER, LIKE SON

☐ COMPLETED SUCCESSFULLY

☐ YET TO DO

☐ CERTIFIED EXPERT

SIGNED WITNESS

NOW GIVE IT A REVIEW

HOW MANY STARS?

☆ ☆ ☆ ☆ ☆

____ OUT OF FIVE

HIGHLY RECOMMENDED ☐

IT WAS ENJOYABLE ☐

NOT WORTH THE TIME ☐

MANDATORY DAD CLICHÉ · LIKE FATHER, LIKE SON

☐ COMPLETED SUCCESSFULLY

☐ YET TO DO

☐ CERTIFIED EXPERT

SIGNED WITNESS

NOW GIVE IT A REVIEW

HOW MANY STARS?

☆ ☆ ☆ ☆ ☆

____ OUT OF FIVE

HIGHLY RECOMMENDED ☐

IT WAS ENJOYABLE ☐

NOT WORTH THE TIME ☐

MANDATORY DAD CLICHÉ · LIKE FATHER, LIKE SON

SIGNED WITNESS

COMPLETED SUCCESSFULLY ☐

YET TO DO ☐

CERTIFIED EXPERT ☐

NOW GIVE IT A REVIEW

☐ HIGHLY RECOMMENDED

☐ IT WAS ENJOYABLE

☐ NOT WORTH THE TIME

HOW MANY STARS?

☆ ☆ ☆ ☆ ☆

___ OUT OF FIVE

MANDATORY DAD CLICHÉ · LIKE FATHER, LIKE SON

SIGNED WITNESS

COMPLETED SUCCESSFULLY ☐

YET TO DO ☐

CERTIFIED EXPERT ☐

NOW GIVE IT A REVIEW

☐ HIGHLY RECOMMENDED

☐ IT WAS ENJOYABLE

☐ NOT WORTH THE TIME

HOW MANY STARS?

☆ ☆ ☆ ☆ ☆

___ OUT OF FIVE

MANDATORY DAD CLICHÉ • LIKE FATHER, LIKE SON

☐ COMPLETED SUCCESSFULLY

☐ YET TO DO

☐ CERTIFIED EXPERT

SIGNED WITNESS

NOW GIVE IT A REVIEW

HOW MANY STARS?

☆ ☆ ☆ ☆ ☆

___ OUT OF FIVE

HIGHLY RECOMMENDED ☐

IT WAS ENJOYABLE ☐

NOT WORTH THE TIME ☐

MANDATORY DAD CLICHÉ • LIKE FATHER, LIKE SON

☐ COMPLETED SUCCESSFULLY

☐ YET TO DO

☐ CERTIFIED EXPERT

SIGNED WITNESS

NOW GIVE IT A REVIEW

HOW MANY STARS?

☆ ☆ ☆ ☆ ☆

___ OUT OF FIVE

HIGHLY RECOMMENDED ☐

IT WAS ENJOYABLE ☐

NOT WORTH THE TIME ☐

MANDATORY DAD CLICHÉ • LIKE FATHER, LIKE SON

SIGNED WITNESS

COMPLETED SUCCESSFULLY ☐

YET TO DO ☐

CERTIFIED EXPERT ☐

NOW GIVE IT A REVIEW

☐ HIGHLY RECOMMENDED

☐ IT WAS ENJOYABLE

☐ NOT WORTH THE TIME

HOW MANY STARS?

☆ ☆ ☆ ☆ ☆

___ OUT OF FIVE

MANDATORY DAD CLICHÉ • LIKE FATHER, LIKE SON

SIGNED WITNESS

COMPLETED SUCCESSFULLY ☐

YET TO DO ☐

CERTIFIED EXPERT ☐

NOW GIVE IT A REVIEW

☐ HIGHLY RECOMMENDED

☐ IT WAS ENJOYABLE

☐ NOT WORTH THE TIME

HOW MANY STARS?

☆ ☆ ☆ ☆ ☆

___ OUT OF FIVE

MANDATORY DAD CLICHÉ • LIKE FATHER, LIKE SON

- [ ] COMPLETED SUCCESSFULLY
- [ ] YET TO DO
- [ ] CERTIFIED EXPERT

SIGNED WITNESS

NOW GIVE IT A REVIEW

HOW MANY STARS?

☆ ☆ ☆ ☆ ☆

___ OUT OF FIVE

- HIGHLY RECOMMENDED [ ]
- IT WAS ENJOYABLE [ ]
- NOT WORTH THE TIME [ ]

MANDATORY DAD CLICHÉ • LIKE FATHER, LIKE SON

- [ ] COMPLETED SUCCESSFULLY
- [ ] YET TO DO
- [ ] CERTIFIED EXPERT

SIGNED WITNESS

NOW GIVE IT A REVIEW

HOW MANY STARS?

☆ ☆ ☆ ☆ ☆

___ OUT OF FIVE

- HIGHLY RECOMMENDED [ ]
- IT WAS ENJOYABLE [ ]
- NOT WORTH THE TIME [ ]

MANDATORY DAD CLICHÉ · LIKE FATHER, LIKE SON

SIGNED WITNESS

COMPLETED SUCCESSFULLY ☐

YET TO DO ☐

CERTIFIED EXPERT ☐

NOW GIVE IT A REVIEW

☐ HIGHLY RECOMMENDED

☐ IT WAS ENJOYABLE

☐ NOT WORTH THE TIME

HOW MANY STARS?

☆ ☆ ☆ ☆ ☆

___ OUT OF FIVE

MANDATORY DAD CLICHÉ · LIKE FATHER, LIKE SON

SIGNED WITNESS

COMPLETED SUCCESSFULLY ☐

YET TO DO ☐

CERTIFIED EXPERT ☐

NOW GIVE IT A REVIEW

☐ HIGHLY RECOMMENDED

☐ IT WAS ENJOYABLE

☐ NOT WORTH THE TIME

HOW MANY STARS?

☆ ☆ ☆ ☆ ☆

___ OUT OF FIVE

MANDATORY DAD CLICHÉ • LIKE FATHER, LIKE SON

- [ ] COMPLETED SUCCESSFULLY
- [ ] YET TO DO
- [ ] CERTIFIED EXPERT

SIGNED WITNESS

NOW GIVE IT A REVIEW

HOW MANY STARS?

☆ ☆ ☆ ☆ ☆

___ OUT OF FIVE

- HIGHLY RECOMMENDED [ ]
- IT WAS ENJOYABLE [ ]
- NOT WORTH THE TIME [ ]

MANDATORY DAD CLICHÉ • LIKE FATHER, LIKE SON

- [ ] COMPLETED SUCCESSFULLY
- [ ] YET TO DO
- [ ] CERTIFIED EXPERT

SIGNED WITNESS

NOW GIVE IT A REVIEW

HOW MANY STARS?

☆ ☆ ☆ ☆ ☆

___ OUT OF FIVE

- HIGHLY RECOMMENDED [ ]
- IT WAS ENJOYABLE [ ]
- NOT WORTH THE TIME [ ]

SURELY WE'VE MISSED SOME WONDERFULLY TERRIBLE THINGS THAT ALL DADS DO. RECORD THEM HERE—AND DON'T CALL US SHIRLEY.

PSST: SHARE THEM WITH US @BRASSMONKEYGOODS

MANDATORY DAD CLICHÉ • NOW IT'S YOUR TURN

☐ COMPLETED SUCCESSFULLY

☐ YET TO DO

☐ CERTIFIED EXPERT

SIGNED WITNESS

NOW GIVE IT A REVIEW

HOW MANY STARS?

☆ ☆ ☆ ☆ ☆

___ OUT OF FIVE

HIGHLY RECOMMENDED ☐

IT WAS ENJOYABLE ☐

NOT WORTH THE TIME ☐

MANDATORY DAD CLICHÉ • NOW IT'S YOUR TURN

☐ COMPLETED SUCCESSFULLY

☐ YET TO DO

☐ CERTIFIED EXPERT

SIGNED WITNESS

NOW GIVE IT A REVIEW

HOW MANY STARS?

☆ ☆ ☆ ☆ ☆

___ OUT OF FIVE

HIGHLY RECOMMENDED ☐

IT WAS ENJOYABLE ☐

NOT WORTH THE TIME ☐

MANDATORY DAD CLICHÉ • NOW IT'S YOUR TURN

SIGNED WITNESS

COMPLETED SUCCESSFULLY ☐

YET TO DO ☐

CERTIFIED EXPERT ☐

NOW GIVE IT A REVIEW

☐ HIGHLY RECOMMENDED

☐ IT WAS ENJOYABLE

☐ NOT WORTH THE TIME

HOW MANY STARS?

☆☆☆☆☆

___ OUT OF FIVE

MANDATORY DAD CLICHÉ • NOW IT'S YOUR TURN

SIGNED WITNESS

COMPLETED SUCCESSFULLY ☐

YET TO DO ☐

CERTIFIED EXPERT ☐

NOW GIVE IT A REVIEW

☐ HIGHLY RECOMMENDED

☐ IT WAS ENJOYABLE

☐ NOT WORTH THE TIME

HOW MANY STARS?

☆☆☆☆☆

___ OUT OF FIVE

MANDATORY DAD CLICHÉ • NOW IT'S YOUR TURN

☐ COMPLETED SUCCESSFULLY

☐ YET TO DO

☐ CERTIFIED EXPERT

SIGNED WITNESS

NOW GIVE IT A REVIEW

HOW MANY STARS?

☆ ☆ ☆ ☆ ☆

___ OUT OF FIVE

HIGHLY RECOMMENDED ☐

IT WAS ENJOYABLE ☐

NOT WORTH THE TIME ☐

MANDATORY DAD CLICHÉ • NOW IT'S YOUR TURN

☐ COMPLETED SUCCESSFULLY

☐ YET TO DO

☐ CERTIFIED EXPERT

SIGNED WITNESS

NOW GIVE IT A REVIEW

HOW MANY STARS?

☆ ☆ ☆ ☆ ☆

___ OUT OF FIVE

HIGHLY RECOMMENDED ☐

IT WAS ENJOYABLE ☐

NOT WORTH THE TIME ☐

MANDATORY DAD CLICHÉ • NOW IT'S YOUR TURN

COMPLETED SUCCESSFULLY ☐

YET TO DO ☐

CERTIFIED EXPERT ☐

SIGNED WITNESS

NOW GIVE IT A REVIEW

☐ HIGHLY RECOMMENDED

☐ IT WAS ENJOYABLE

☐ NOT WORTH THE TIME

HOW MANY STARS?

☆☆☆☆☆

___ OUT OF FIVE

MANDATORY DAD CLICHÉ • NOW IT'S YOUR TURN

COMPLETED SUCCESSFULLY ☐

YET TO DO ☐

CERTIFIED EXPERT ☐

SIGNED WITNESS

NOW GIVE IT A REVIEW

☐ HIGHLY RECOMMENDED

☐ IT WAS ENJOYABLE

☐ NOT WORTH THE TIME

HOW MANY STARS?

☆☆☆☆☆

___ OUT OF FIVE

MANDATORY DAD CLICHÉ • NOW IT'S YOUR TURN

COMPLETED SUCCESSFULLY

YET TO DO

CERTIFIED EXPERT

SIGNED WITNESS

NOW GIVE IT A REVIEW

HOW MANY STARS?

☆ ☆ ☆ ☆ ☆

___ OUT OF FIVE

HIGHLY RECOMMENDED

IT WAS ENJOYABLE

NOT WORTH THE TIME

MANDATORY DAD CLICHÉ • NOW IT'S YOUR TURN

COMPLETED SUCCESSFULLY

YET TO DO

CERTIFIED EXPERT

SIGNED WITNESS

NOW GIVE IT A REVIEW

HOW MANY STARS?

☆ ☆ ☆ ☆ ☆

___ OUT OF FIVE

HIGHLY RECOMMENDED

IT WAS ENJOYABLE

NOT WORTH THE TIME

MANDATORY DAD CLICHÉ • NOW IT'S YOUR TURN

SIGNED WITNESS

COMPLETED SUCCESSFULLY ☐

YET TO DO ☐

CERTIFIED EXPERT ☐

NOW GIVE IT A REVIEW

☐ HIGHLY RECOMMENDED

☐ IT WAS ENJOYABLE

☐ NOT WORTH THE TIME

HOW MANY STARS?

☆ ☆ ☆ ☆ ☆

___ OUT OF FIVE

MANDATORY DAD CLICHÉ • NOW IT'S YOUR TURN

SIGNED WITNESS

COMPLETED SUCCESSFULLY ☐

YET TO DO ☐

CERTIFIED EXPERT ☐

NOW GIVE IT A REVIEW

☐ HIGHLY RECOMMENDED

☐ IT WAS ENJOYABLE

☐ NOT WORTH THE TIME

HOW MANY STARS?

☆ ☆ ☆ ☆ ☆

___ OUT OF FIVE

BRASSMONKEYGOODS.COM

✕

@BRASSMONKEYGOODS 📷